rāma jayam - likhita japam

⸭

rāma-nāma mālā
upon hanumān chālisā

⁚

A Rama-Nama Journal
for
Writing the 'Rama' Name 100,000 Times
upon Hanuman Chalisa

राम जयम - लिखित जपम

⸭

हनुमान चालीसा पर राम-नाम माला

⁚

राम-नाम लेखन पुस्तिका
(एक लाख नाम हेतु)

Belongs to _____

Published by: **Rama-Nama Journals**
(an Imprint of e1i1 Corporation)

Title: **Rama Jayam - Likhita Japam :: Rama-Nama Mala Upon Hanuman Chalisa**
Sub-Title: A Rama-Nama Journal for Writing the 'Rama' Name 100,000 Times upon Hanuman Chalisa

Author: **Sushma**

Parts of this book have been derived/inspired from our other publication:
"Rama Hymns" (Authored by Sushma)

<u>Identifiers</u>

ISBN: **978-1-945739-16-3** (Paperback)

—o—

—o—

www.**e1i1**.com -- www.**OnlyRama**.com
email: **e1i1**bookse1i1@gmail.com

Our books can be bought online, or at Amazon, or any bookstore. If a book is not available at your neighborhood bookstore they will be happy to order it for you. (Certain Hardcover Editions may not be immediately available—we apologize)

Some of our Current/Forthcoming Books are listed below. Please note that this is a partial list and that we are continually adding new books. Please visit www.**e1i1**.com / www.**onlyRama**.com for current offerings.

- **Tulsi Ramayana—The Hindu Bible:** Ramcharitmanas with English Translation & Transliteration
- **Ramcharitmanas:** Ramayana of Tulsidas with Transliteration (in English)
- **Ramayana, Large:** Tulsi Ramcharitmanas, Hindi only Edition, Large Font and Paper size
- **Ramayana, Medium:** Tulsi Ramcharitmanas, Hindi only Edition, Medium Font and Paper size
- **Ramayana, Small:** Tulsi Ramcharitmanas, Hindi only Edition, Small Font and Paper size
- **Sundarakanda:** The Fifth-Ascent of Tulsi Ramayana
- **RAMA GOD:** In the Beginning - Upanishad Vidya (Know Thyself)
- **Purling Shadows:** And A Dream Called Life - Upanishad Vidya (Know Thyself)
- **Fiery Circle:** Upanishad Vidya (Know Thyself)
- **Rama Hymns:** Hanuman-Chalisa, Rāma-Raksha-Stotra, Bhushumdi-Ramayana, Nama-Ramayanam, Rāma-Shata-Nama-Stotra, etc. with Transliteration & English Translation
- **Rama Jayam - Likhita Japam :: Rama-Nama Mala** (several): Rama-Nama Journals for Writing the 'Rama' Name 100,000 Times
- **Tulsi-Ramayana Rama-Nama Mala** (multiple volumes): Legacy Journals for Writing the Rama Name along with Tulsi Ramayana

-- On our website may be found links to renditions of Rama Hymns –

-- Rama Mantras/Hymns/Pictures are also available printed on Quality Shirts from Amazon. See our website for details --

rāma-nāma mahimā

In this modern era—which is awash with the six *Gunas* of Māyā: *Kāma* (Lust), *Krodha* (Anger), *Lobha* (Greed), *Moha* (Infatuation), *Mada* (Pride) & *Mātsarya* (Envy)—we find our minds sinking in worldliness. It seems that no one can remain unsullied from the taints of Kali despite their best intent; this seems to be the fait-accompli of the *Kali-Yuga*—a very sad fate indeed. But despair not, because there is hope—we find ourselves assured.

The Japa of Rāma-Nāma (Rāma-Name) is the supreme path to salvation in this *Kali-Yuga*, assure our Scriptures; there is no Dharma higher than Nāma-Dharma in this Age of Kali—we are told. Sing the praises of the Lord and remain engaged in *Nāma-Smarana*—is the advice given to us by our saints. The chanting of Rāma-Nāma is The-One-Supreme-Path to escape the clutches of *Kali-Yuga*—declares Rāmacharitmānas—and in fact it is the one and only Dharma which is easy and feasible in the present times.

Many of the Hindu saints zealously assert: "In this Kali-Yuga, there is no other means, no other means, no other means of salvation—other than chanting the holy name Rāma, chanting the holy name Rāma, chanting the holy name Rāma."

Rāma-Japa—the constant repetition of the Supreme-Mantra 'Rāma'—is usually done mentally, or on a rosary; but there is one extremely efficacious method of this Japa: the *Likhita-Japa*, or the Written-Chant.

The practice of writing the Rāma Mantra over and over on paper is called the *Likhita-Japa*. This written form of Japa is a lasting record of your chant, remaining ever imbued with those holy vibrations, for all times, for the benefit of you and the future generations.

In India, as you may know, devotees of God have been chanting the name 'Rāma' and writing the Name 'Rāma'—pages upon pages of it, running into billions and billions, for ages. Hindu children are taught to write the Rāma-Nāma from their very childhood, and the writing competitions of the One *Lakh* Rāma–Nāma, brings up nostalgic memories for many Hindus.

The completed Rāma-Nāma books are variously utilized. Some devotees preserve them carefully for their holy association and divine energy, while others donate them to temples. The written Rāma-Nāma Books are used in the foundations of temples during construction; they add divine energy to the Temples—while in turn strengthening the foundations of the spiritual life of those who wrote the Rāma Name. Also some collected Rāma-Nāma books are placed in crypts to be used during *Yagna's* in Rāma Temples; and temples preserve these books for future. Devotees also place their own written Rāma-Nāma Books during the laying of foundation of their new homes, or in their *Pooja*-Room.

Of those of our Chakras (psychic centers), where our *Sanchit* (accumulated) Karmas are stored, Rāma is the *Beej Mantra*. The writing of Rāma-Nāma helps cleanse the Chakras, and our suppressed emotions, and the negative *Sanskaras* of the subconscious, and our remnant/unworked Karmas from past lives—which all get purged through the repetition of the Rāma-Nāma Mantra.

The chanting of Rāma-Nāma is a direct way to liberation. As per belief, devotees attempt to write down at least Eighty-Four Lakh (84,00,000) Rāma-Nāmas to get out of the birth-death cycle of Eighty-Four Lakh *Yonīs*, and thereby attain to salvation.

The *Likhita* Rāma-Nāma Japa is a powerful and transformative tool. As you write the Rāma-Nāma, all the senses become engaged in the service of Lord-God, and you find yourself simultaneously chanting and hearing and contemplating on the Lord—everything comes together naturally. This method clears away your thoughts and helps concentrate the entirety of your soul upon the Divine.

Any Japa is beneficial but somehow writing the Rāma-Nāma on paper brings up a great singularity of focus within the mind—and the peace of heart which ensues is something which is not so easily achieved with other forms of Japa. The written form of Rāma-Japa is somehow able to engage those parts of our body-mind continuum which other methods can not—and our meditative stance is able to achieve much deeper levels.

There is something special which will happen when you write the Rāma-Nāma—as you will discover. Peace and tranquility will surround you as you write the Supreme-Mantra: Rāma. The Rāma-Nāma will impart to you supreme strength, and great tolerance to withstand the vicissitudes of life. Bright unclouded wisdom will illumine your mind. You will find yourself in complete sense of surrender to your inner being. The resonance of God will resonate throughout your mind-body continuity. You will feel a flux of divine energy resonating within you. You will get great power and peace in your everyday life. The chanting of Rāma Mantra will protect your inner world as well as the outside.

Although the Rāma-Mantra is the gateway to higher consciousness and spiritual upliftment, but even at such junctures—when you find yourself in odd situations, where all the paths seem blocked—then just walking away from everything and simply writing the Rāma Nāma, will give you much needed clarity of thought—and a divine inspiration that will show the way out.

Thus, the Rāma Nāma is very transformative: with it you gain a balanced progress in your outside world and the inner. *Sant* Tulsidās says in *Rāmacharitmānas*: Place the Rāma-Nāma Jewel at the threshold, and there will be light both inside and out; i.e. a constant chant of the Rāma-Nāma from the mouth—the doorway to the body—will bring you external materialistic wellbeing, and also an inner spiritual wellness—both. Incredibly, with the Rāma-Nāma, you get to have the best of both the worlds.

According to the Vedas, just as the sun dispels the darkness, the chanting of Rāma-Nāma dispels all the evils and obstacles of life. The Rāma Nāma cures agony and showers the blessings of God; all righteous wishes get fulfilled; jealousy and pride disappear; life becomes imbued with satisfaction and peace; all of life's needs fall in place automatically—just like a miracle of nature guiding nature's forces. You may not always get what you want in the exact same form, but the Rāma-Nāma will purify things and bring to you the same needed happiness and bliss in a much more refined and lasting way. Your life will truly become filled with tranquility. Thus, with the Rāma-Nāma, an immense sense of spiritual wellbeing is experienced apart from gain of material happiness.

For *Likhita* Japa, you can write the Rāma-Nāma in any language of your choice—after all, Name is the connecting chord between the Divine and your inner self—but writing the Rāma-Nāma in its original Sanskrit form is simply superlative—most excellent. Sanskrit is *Deva-Bhāshā* (the language-of-gods). If you do not know how to write राम in Sanskrit it is quite easy. In the figure below, trace the contours 1-2 (which is the sound of underlined letters in the word '**ru**n'), 3-4 (the sound of underlined letter **a** in '**a**rk'), 5-6 & 7-8 (the underlined **mu** in '**mu**st') and lastly the line 9-10; and that's it. Note the similarity of English **R** , **M** to the Sanskrit र , म , (and English words used here like *Name, Saint*—similar to the Sanskrit *Nāma, Sant.*) All European languages have their roots in Sanskrit, the mother tongue of humanity.

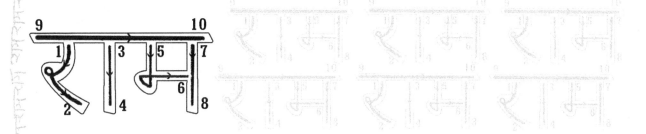

Write the Supreme-Mantra Rāma with reverence, every day, preferably at a set time, or as and when possible, in small measures, or copiously—howsoever your situation permits. There are no hard rules, do what feels good to your Soul. The important thing is to engage in the *Likhita*-Japa. When completed, you could keep the books in your Worship-Room, preserve them as treasures to pass on to future generations, donate them to Rāma Temples, or gift them to your loved ones—who will thereby inculcate crucial values from you, and learn the importance of the Rāma-Nāma, and get inspired with Hindu Values, especially so the younger ones.

While writing, focus your mind on the Rāma-Name and chant it within. Imagine Sītā-Rāma showering you with their bliss. Try to stay free of distractions, and with time you will find that your mind will take a natural meditative stance while engaged in the written Rāma-Nāma Japa.

You can choose any notebook or paper to write on, not necessarily this one. Traditionally people will write the Rāma Name in red ink on straight lines; but some devotees will also simultaneously make an interesting design—by changing the orientation of lines, or using different colors, utilizing an underlying outline to base their Japa upon. Do what comes naturally; no hard rules.

Find a set of pencils or pens which write and feel beautiful to you. If making an intricate pattern use pens that have finer points—but see that the ink does not bleed through to the other side.

Ideally, you will have a special set of pens kept purely for the Likhita Japa. This will make it easier for you to enter into the spirit of things. You will find that such implements—which you habitually use for holy tasks—build up energy and holy resonance.

A grid of 21 by 48 (1008 boxes) is provided for you to be able to write a thousand Rāma Names per page. With 108 pages to write upon, and with space for 1008 names per page, you should be able to cross the 100,000 Rāma-Nāma objective of the book. The 100,000 target is merely suggestive—it assumes you write one Rāma-Nāma per box; obviously your mileage will vary, and you will get a figure more or less than 100,000 depending upon if you write smaller or larger. If need be, please utilize the empty spaces below the page or to the side.

The grid is provided simply as a guide—most people tend to ignore the boxes and write in their own style, as and how their own inspiration leads them, creating their own design on the pages. The pages contain the Hanuman-Chalisa Text as font outlines. Before beginning your Likhita Japa for that page, if you can write within the Chalisa outlines the Rama-Namas—using color/size/slant which is different from the outside—then it will make the Verses stand out. Or if you cannot write so tiny, then simply color the verses using colored pencil or highlighter—that way the Text will pop out from amongst the waves of surrounding Rāma-Nāmas. We wish you Happy Rāma-Nāma Japa.

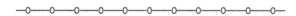

This Rāma-Nāma Mālā Journal has the underlying Hanuman-Chalisa Text. Other Journals in the Series have outlines of other Important Devotional Texts around which you can write the 100,000 Rāma-Nāmas. Where space is limited, the Text Outlines are only in Sanskrit; however, original text, transliteration & translation is also provided in regular font on each set of pages. All these Journals are available online, or please go to your local bookstore and they can get these for you.

Title: Rama Jayam - Likhita Japam :: Rama-Nama Mala, Simple I,II,III...
Title: Rama Jayam - Likhita Japam :: Rama-Nama Mala Upon Rama Raksha Stotra
Title: Rama Jayam - Likhita Japam :: Rama-Nama Mala Upon Nama-Ramayanam
Title: Rama Jayam - Likhita Japam :: Rama-Nama Mala Upon Rama 108 Names
Title: Rama Jayam - Likhita Japam :: Rama-Nama Mala Upon Ramashtakam
... and many more on the way

Our following Journal:
Tulsi-Ramayana Rama-Nama Mala (in multiple volumes): Legacy Journals for Writing the Rama Name along with Full Tulsi Ramayana, is a legacy Journal in which you can write down your spiritual sentiments, and the Rāma-Nāma, alongside the printed Tulsi Ramayana. The book contains the original text, transliteration, translation, and space for you to jot down your thoughts and write the Rama-Nama. Pages also have inspirational words of Hindu Saint to help guide aspirants on their spiritual journey. You can embellish the entire Tulsi Ramayana with your Rama-Namas and gift them to your loved ones—a truly unique gift of love, care, labor, and devotion.

If interested, you can now buy Quality Shirts from Amazon with printed Important Rāma-Hymn Texts like: Hanumān Chālisā, Sundarakānda, Kishkindhākānda, Rāma-Rakshā-Stotra, Nāma-Rāmayanam, Rāma-Shata-Nāma-Stotra etc.

राम
राम
राम
राम
राम
राम
राम
राम
राम
राम
राम
राम
राम
राम
राम
राम
राम
राम
राम
राम
राम
राम
राम
राम
राम
राम
राम
राम
राम
राम
राम
राम
राम
राम
राम
राम
राम
राम
राम
राम

जय हनुमान

जय सीताराम

श्रीगुरु चरन

सरोज रज

śrīguru
carana saroja
raja

राम
राम
राम
राम
राम
राम
राम
राम
राम
राम
राम
राम
राम
राम
राम
राम
राम
राम
राम
राम
राम
राम
राम
राम
राम
राम
राम
राम
राम
राम
राम
राम
राम
राम
राम
राम
राम
राम
राम

: Today's Date :

राम राम

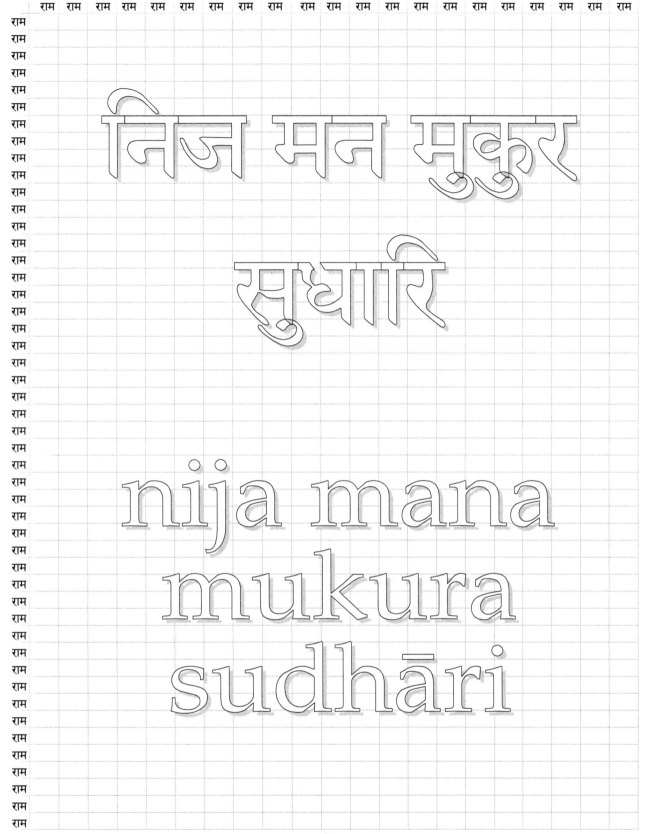

निज मन मुकुर सुधारि

nija mana mukura sudhāri

श्रीगुरु चरन सरोज रज निज मन मुकुर सुधारि ।
śrīguru carana saroja raja nija mana mukura sudhāri,
Cleansing the mirror of mind with the dust from the lotus feet of the revered Guru,

बरनउँ रघुबर

विमल जस

baranaūṁ
raghubara
bimala jasa

राम
राम
राम
राम
राम
राम
राम
राम
राम
राम
राम
राम
राम
राम
राम
राम
राम
राम
राम
राम
राम
राम
राम
राम
राम
राम
राम
राम
राम
राम
राम
राम
राम
राम
राम
राम
राम
राम
राम

Today's Date :

राम
राम
राम
राम
राम
राम
राम
राम
राम
राम
राम
राम
राम
राम
राम
राम
राम
राम
राम
राम
राम
राम
राम
राम
राम
राम
राम
राम
राम
राम
राम
राम
राम
राम
राम
राम
राम
राम
राम
राम
राम

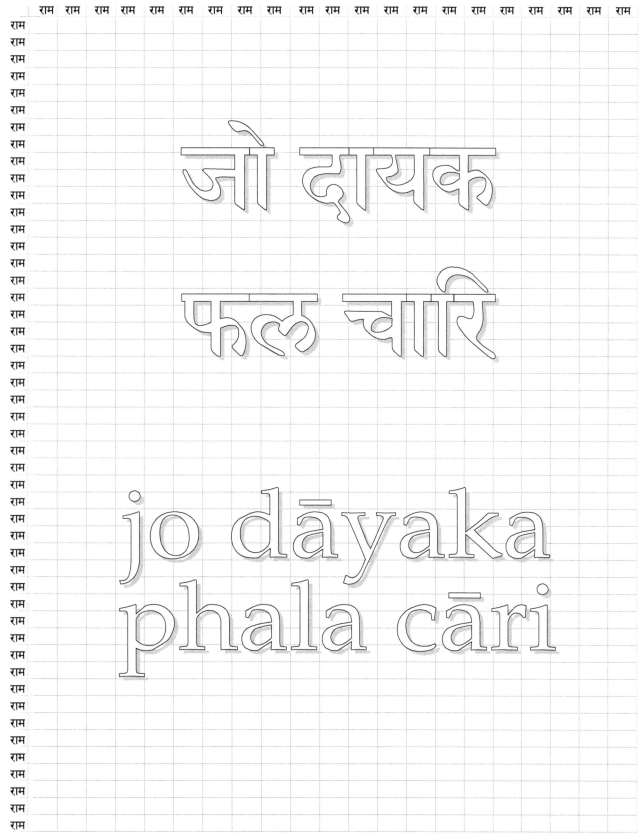

बरनउँ रघुबर बिमल जस जो दायक फल चारि ॥
baranaūṁ raghubara bimala jasa jo dāyaka phala cāri.
I sing the unsullied glories of Shrī Rāma—the bestower of four fruits of life.

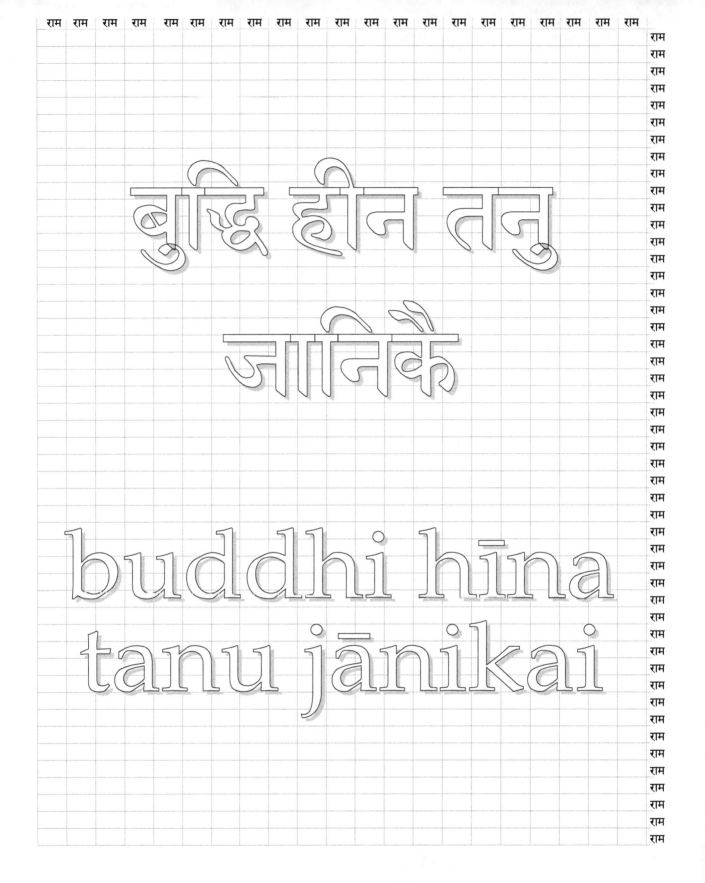

बुद्धि हीन तनु
जानिकै

buddhi hīna
tanu jānikai

राम
राम
राम
राम
राम
राम
राम
राम
राम
राम
राम
राम
राम
राम
राम
राम
राम
राम
राम
राम
राम
राम
राम
राम
राम
राम
राम
राम
राम
राम
राम
राम
राम
राम
राम
राम
राम
राम

: Today's Date :

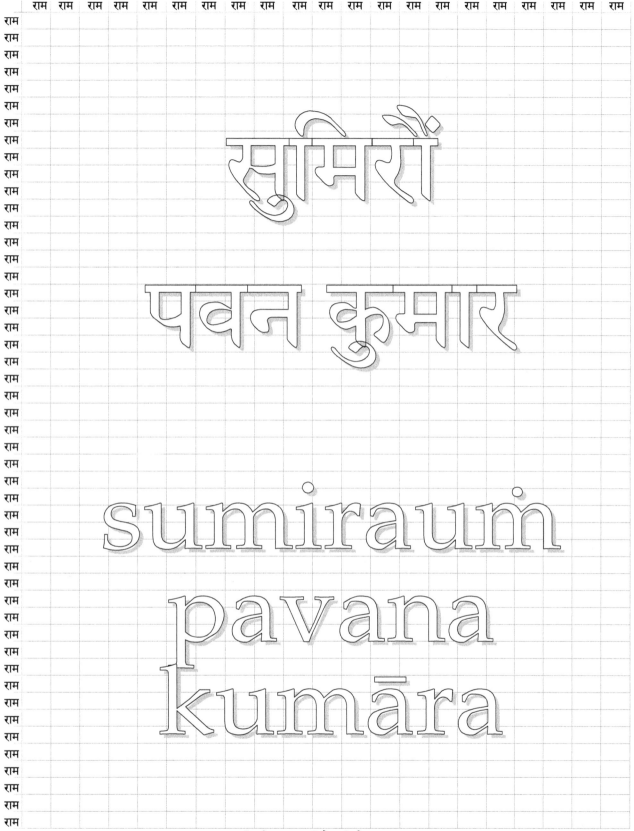

बुद्धि हीन तनु जानिकै सुमिरौं पवन कुमार ।
buddhi hīna tanu jānikai sumirauṁ pavana kumāra,
Knowing this material body to be void of intelligence and seeped in ignorance, I meditate on the Son-of-Wind seeking his favor:

: Today's Date :

. 7 .

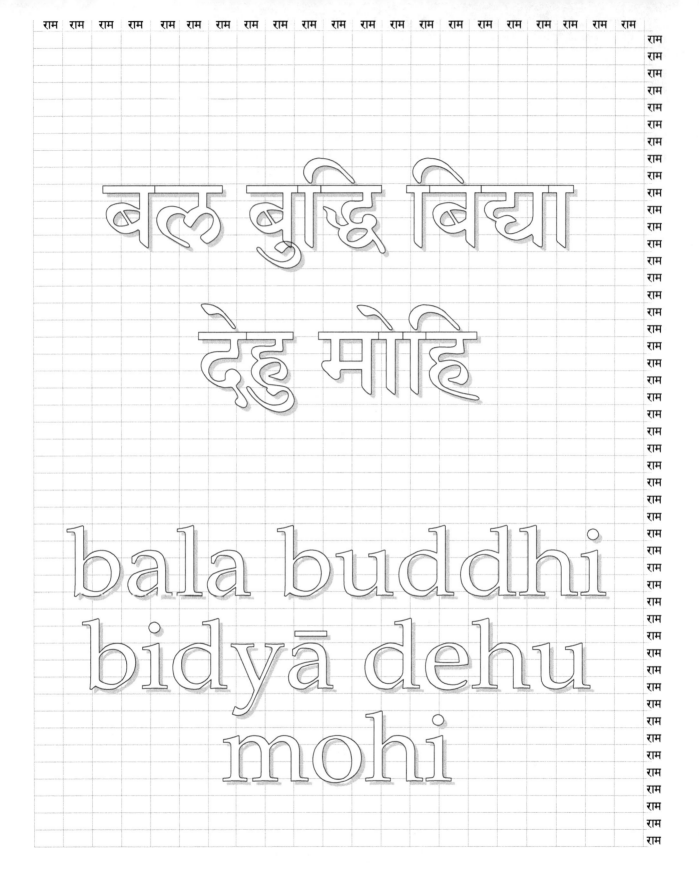

बल बुद्धि बिद्या
देहु मोहि

bala buddhi
bidyā dehu
mohi

राम
राम
राम
राम
राम
राम
राम
राम
राम
राम
राम
राम
राम
राम
राम
राम
राम
राम
राम
राम
राम
राम
राम
राम
राम
राम
राम
राम
राम
राम
राम
राम
राम
राम
राम
राम
राम
राम

Today's Date :

बल बुद्धि बिद्या देहु मोहि हरहु कलेश विकार ॥
bala buddhi bidyā dehu mohi harahu kaleśa vikāra.
Impart to me strength, intelligence, virtuosity; and remove all ailments and imperfections, my Lord.

जय हनुमान

ज्ञान गुण सागर

jaya
hanumāna
jñāna guṇa
sāgara

राम
राम
राम
राम
राम
राम
राम
राम
राम
राम
राम
राम
राम
राम
राम
राम
राम
राम
राम
राम
राम
राम
राम
राम
राम
राम
राम
राम
राम
राम
राम
राम
राम
राम
राम
राम
राम

: Today's Date :

राम
राम
राम
राम
राम
राम
राम
राम
राम
राम
राम
राम
राम
राम
राम
राम
राम
राम
राम
राम
राम
राम
राम
राम
राम
राम
राम
राम
राम
राम
राम
राम
राम

जय कपीश

तिहुँ लोक उजागर

jaya kapīśa
tihuṃ loka
ujāgara

चौपाई - caupāī

जय हनुमान ज्ञान गुण सागर । जय कपीश तिहुँ लोक उजागर ॥

jaya hanumāna jñāna guṇa sāgara, jaya kapīśa tihuṃ loka ujāgara. 1.

Glory be to Hanumān—the ocean of wisdom and virtues. Victory to the monkey-god whose
resplendency irradiates the three spheres of creation.

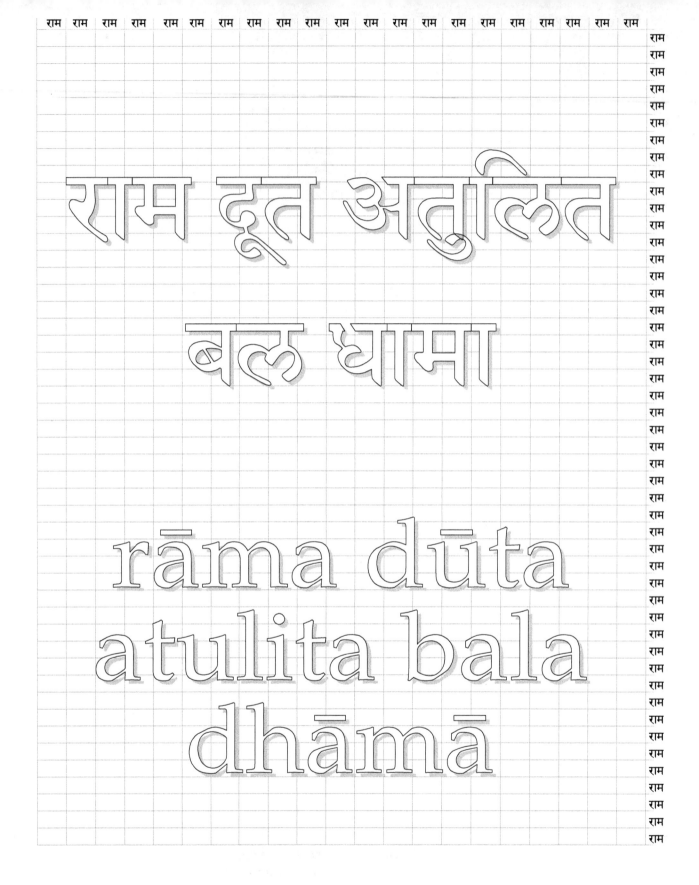

राम दूत अतुलित

बल धामा

rāma dūta

atulita bala

dhāmā

राम
राम
राम
राम
राम
राम
राम
राम
राम
राम
राम
राम
राम
राम
राम
राम
राम
राम
राम
राम
राम
राम
राम
राम
राम
राम
राम
राम
राम
राम
राम
राम
राम
राम
राम
राम
राम

राम दूत अतुलित बल धामा **।** अंजनिपुत्र पवनसुत नामा **॥**
rāma dūta atulita bala dhāmā, amjani-putra pavanasuta nāmā. 2.
Glory be to the divine messenger and servant of Shrī Rāma, the repository of immeasurable strength.
Glory be to mother Anjani's boy, bearing the name Pavana-Suth—Son-of-Wind.

महाबीर

विक्रम बजरंगी

mahābīra

bikrama

bajaraṁgī

राम
राम
राम
राम
राम
राम
राम
राम
राम
राम
राम
राम
राम
राम
राम
राम
राम
राम
राम
राम
राम
राम
राम
राम
राम
राम
राम
राम
राम
राम
राम
राम
राम
राम
राम
राम

: Today's Date :

राम
राम
राम
राम
राम
राम
राम
राम
राम
राम
राम
राम
राम
राम
राम
राम
राम
राम
राम
राम
राम
राम
राम
राम
राम
राम
राम
राम
राम
राम
राम
राम
राम
राम
राम
राम
राम

महाबीर बिक्रम बजरंगी ꠶ कुमति निवार सुमति के संगी ॥

mahābīra bikrama bajaraṁgī, kumati nivāra sumati ke saṁgī. 3.

O supremely valorous hero of wondrous great deeds, with a body that is strong as diamond: evilness of the mind you cure; a companion you are of those with minds good and pure.

कंचन बरन

बिराज सुबेषा

kaṁcana barana birāja subeṣā

राम
राम
राम
राम
राम
राम
राम
राम
राम
राम
राम
राम
राम
राम
राम
राम
राम
राम
राम
राम
राम
राम
राम
राम
राम
राम
राम
राम
राम
राम
राम
राम
राम
राम
राम
राम
राम
राम

राम
राम
राम
राम
राम
राम
राम
राम
राम
राम
राम
राम
राम
राम
राम
राम
राम
राम
राम
राम
राम
राम
राम
राम
राम
राम
राम
राम
राम
राम
राम
राम
राम
राम

कानन कुंडल
कुंचित केशा

kānana
kuṁḍala
kuṁcita keśā

कंचन बरन बिराज सुबेषा । कानन कुंडल कुंचित केशा ॥
kaṁcana barana birāja subeṣā, kānana kuṁḍala kuṁcita keśā. 4.
With a complexion that's molten gold, you shine resplendent in your exquisite form—with rings in your
ears and lovely curly locks.

हाथ वज्र और
ध्वजा विराजै

hātha bajra
aura dhvajā
birājai

राम
राम
राम
राम
राम
राम
राम
राम
राम
राम
राम
राम
राम
राम
राम
राम
राम
राम
राम
राम
राम
राम
राम
राम
राम
राम
राम
राम
राम
राम
राम
राम
राम
राम
राम
राम
राम

काँधे मूँज

जनेऊ साजै

kāṃ́dhe

mūṃ́ja janeū

sājai

हाथ बज्र और ध्वजा बिराजै । काँधे मूँज जनेऊ साजै ॥
hātha bajra aura dhvajā birājai, kāṃ́dhe mūṃ́ja janeū sājai. 5.
In your hands are held a mace and flag; and there's *Munji* and *Janeu* embellished across your shoulders, well adorned.

शङ्कर स्वयं
केशरीनंदन

śaṅkara
svayaṁ
keśarī
naṁdana

राम
राम
राम
राम
राम
राम
राम
राम
राम
राम
राम
राम
राम
राम
राम
राम
राम
राम
राम
राम
राम
राम
राम
राम
राम
राम
राम
राम
राम
राम
राम
राम
राम
राम
राम
राम
राम
राम
राम
राम
राम
राम
राम
राम
राम
राम

राम
राम
राम
राम
राम
राम
राम
राम
राम
राम
राम
राम
राम
राम
राम
राम
राम
राम
राम
राम
राम
राम
राम
राम
राम
राम
राम
राम
राम
राम
राम
राम
राम
राम
राम
राम
राम
राम

शङ्कर स्वयं केशरीनंदन ꘃ तेज प्रताप महा जग बंदन ॥

śaṅkara svayaṁ keśarīnaṁdana, teja pratāpa mahā jaga baṁdana. 6.

You are Shankar himself (embodied as Hanuman), born to the mighty Keshari—the delight of his heart.
Your majesty and prowess is astounding—venerated throughout the universe.

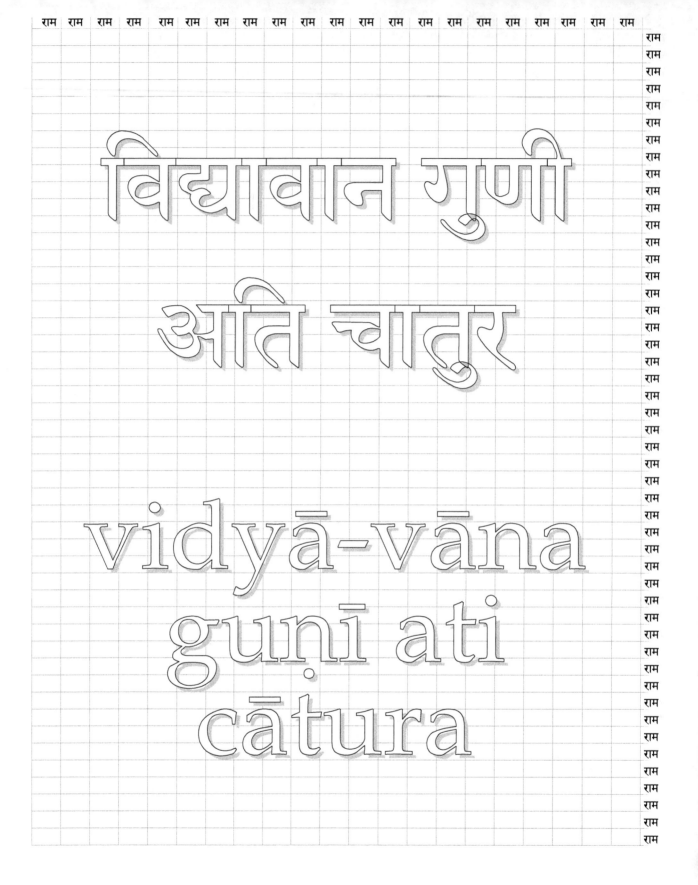

विद्यावान गुणी

अति चातुर

vidyā-vāna
guṇī ati
cātura

राम
राम
राम
राम
राम
राम
राम
राम
राम
राम
राम
राम
राम
राम
राम
राम
राम
राम
राम
राम
राम
राम
राम
राम
राम
राम
राम
राम
राम
राम
राम
राम
राम
राम
राम
राम
राम
राम
राम
राम
राम
राम

राम
राम
राम
राम
राम
राम
राम
राम
राम
राम
राम
राम
राम
राम
राम
राम
राम
राम
राम
राम
राम
राम
राम
राम
राम
राम
राम
राम
राम
राम
राम
राम
राम
राम
राम
राम

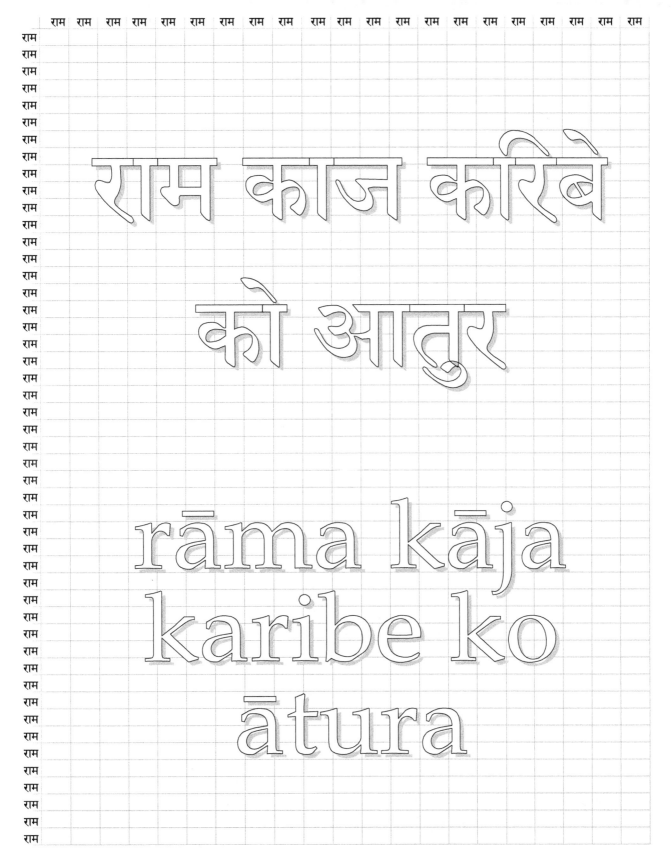

विद्यावान गुणी अति चातुर । राम काज करिबे को आतुर ॥

vidyā-vāna guṇī ati cātura, rāma kāja karibe ko ātura. 7.

Learned in all the sciences, virtuous, most clever and wise—you are ever so eager to do Rāma's tasks.

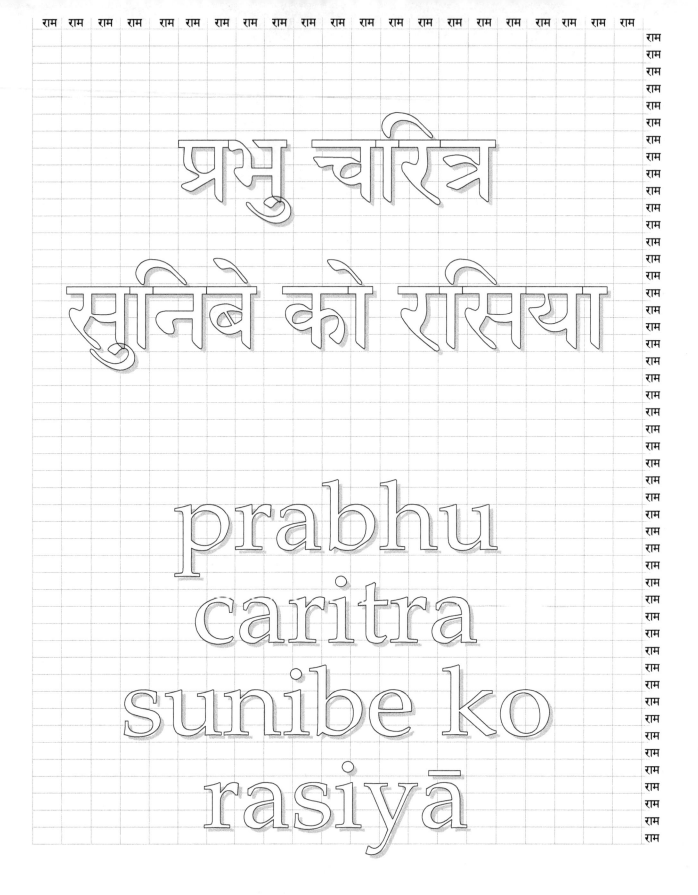

प्रभु चरित्र
सुनिबे को रसिया

prabhu
caritra
sunibe ko
rasiyā

राम लखन सीता मन बसिया

rāma lakhana sītā mana basiyā

प्रभु चरित्र सुनिबे को रसिया ꘡ राम लखन सीता मन बसिया ꘡꘡

prabhu caritra sunibe ko rasiyā, rāma lakhana sītā mana basiyā. 8.

Your greatest delight is in listening to the glories of the Lord, and Rāma-Lakshman-Sītā ever reside in your heart; nay—you ever abide in the hearts of Lakshman-Sītā-Rāma.

सूक्ष्म रूप धरि
सियहि दिखावा

sūkṣma rūpa
dhari siyahiṃ
dikhāvā

राम
राम
राम
राम
राम
राम
राम
राम
राम
राम
राम
राम
राम
राम
राम
राम
राम
राम
राम
राम
राम
राम
राम
राम
राम
राम
राम
राम
राम
राम
राम
राम
राम
राम
राम
राम
राम
राम
राम

राम
राम
राम
राम
राम
राम
राम
राम
राम
राम
राम
राम
राम
राम
राम
राम
राम
राम
राम
राम
राम
राम
राम
राम
राम
राम
राम
राम
राम
राम
राम
राम
राम
राम
राम

बिकट रूप धरि

लंक जरावा

bikaṭa rūpa
dhari laṁka
jarāvā

सूक्ष्म रूप धरि सियहि दिखावा । बिकट रूप धरि लंक जरावा ॥
sūkṣma rūpa dhari siyahiṁ dikhāvā, bikaṭa rūpa dhari laṁka jarāvā. 9.
When visiting mother Sītā you showed yourself in tiny diminutive form; then growing to fearsome
colossal size you burnt the whole of Lankā down;

भीम रूप धरि
असुर सँहारे

bhīma rūpa
dhari asura
saṁhāre

भीम रूप धरि असुर सँहारे । रामचन्द्र के काज सँवारे ॥
bhīma rūpa dhari asura saṁhāre, rāma-candra ke kāja saṁvāre. 10.
assuming a valorous form you destroyed many demons—thus you ever serve to facilitate the works of
the Lord-God Shrī Rāma-Chandra.

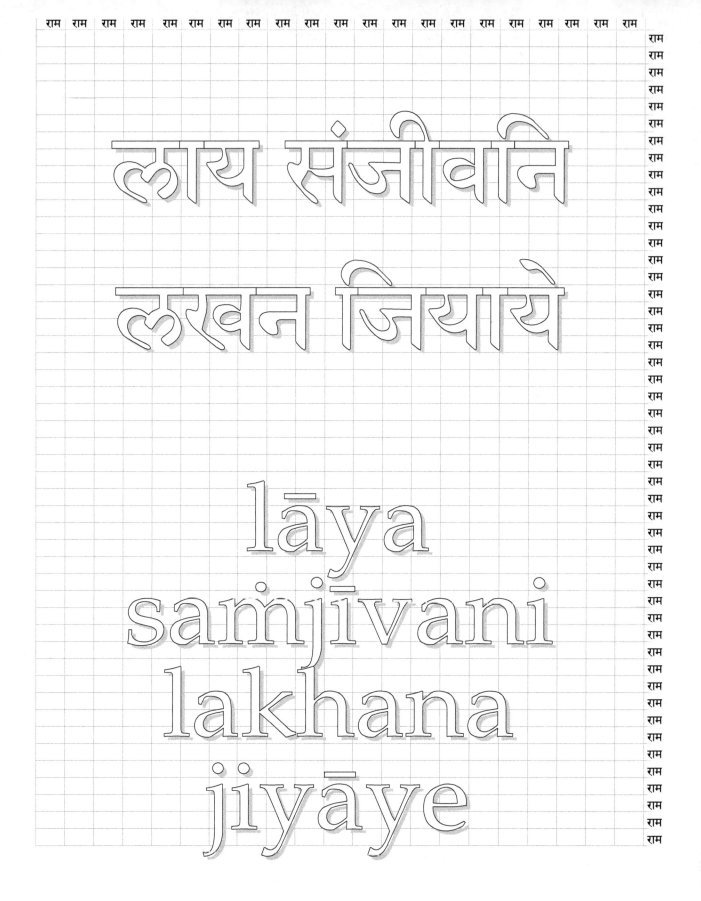

लाय संजीवनि

लखन जियाये

lāya

saṁjīvani

lakhana

jīyāye

: Today's Date :

राम
राम
राम
राम
राम
राम
राम
राम
राम
राम
राम
राम
राम
राम
राम
राम
राम
राम
राम
राम
राम
राम
राम
राम
राम
राम
राम
राम
राम
राम
राम
राम
राम
राम
राम
राम
राम

राम
राम
राम
राम
राम
राम
राम
राम
राम
राम
राम
राम
राम
राम
राम
राम
राम
राम
राम
राम
राम
राम
राम
राम
राम
राम
राम
राम
राम
राम
राम
राम
राम

श्री रघुबीर

हरषि उर लाये

śrī raghu-bīra haraṣi ura lāye

लाय संजीवनि लखन जियाये ꠰ श्री रघुबीर हरषि उर लाये ॥

lāya saṁjīvani lakhana jiyāye, śrī raghu-bīra haraṣi ura lāye. 11.

You brought the *Sanjīvani* and brought Lakshman back to life, whereupon Shrī Rāma embraced you with a heart full of joy.

राम
राम
राम
राम
राम
राम
राम
राम
राम
राम
राम
राम
राम
राम
राम
राम
राम
राम
राम
राम
राम
राम
राम
राम
राम
राम
राम
राम
राम
राम
राम
राम
राम
राम
राम
राम
राम

रघुपति कीन्ही

बहुत बड़ाई

raghupati kinhī

bahuta baṛāī

: Today's Date :

राम
राम
राम
राम
राम
राम
राम
राम
राम
राम
राम
राम
राम
राम
राम
राम
राम
राम
राम
राम
राम
राम
राम
राम
राम
राम
राम
राम
राम
राम
राम
राम
राम
राम
राम
राम
राम

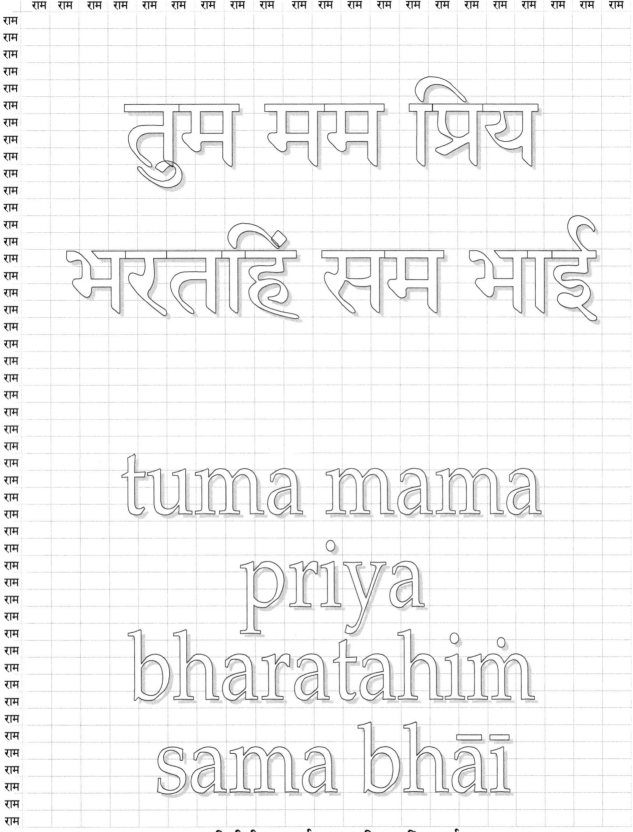

रघुपति कीन्ही बहुत बड़ाई ꠰ तुम मम प्रिय भरतहिं सम भाई ꠱꠱

raghupati kīnhī bahuta baṛāī, tuma mama priya bharatahiṁ sama bhāī. 12.

Rāma, King of Raghus, extolled you profusely and then He proclaimed: You are to me just like Bharata, dear brother of mine.

सहस बदन

तुम्हरो जस गावैं

sahasa badana

tumharo jasa

gāvaiṁ

राम
राम
राम
राम
राम
राम
राम
राम
राम
राम
राम
राम
राम
राम
राम
राम
राम
राम
राम
राम
राम
राम
राम
राम
राम
राम
राम
राम
राम
राम
राम
राम
राम
राम
राम
राम
राम

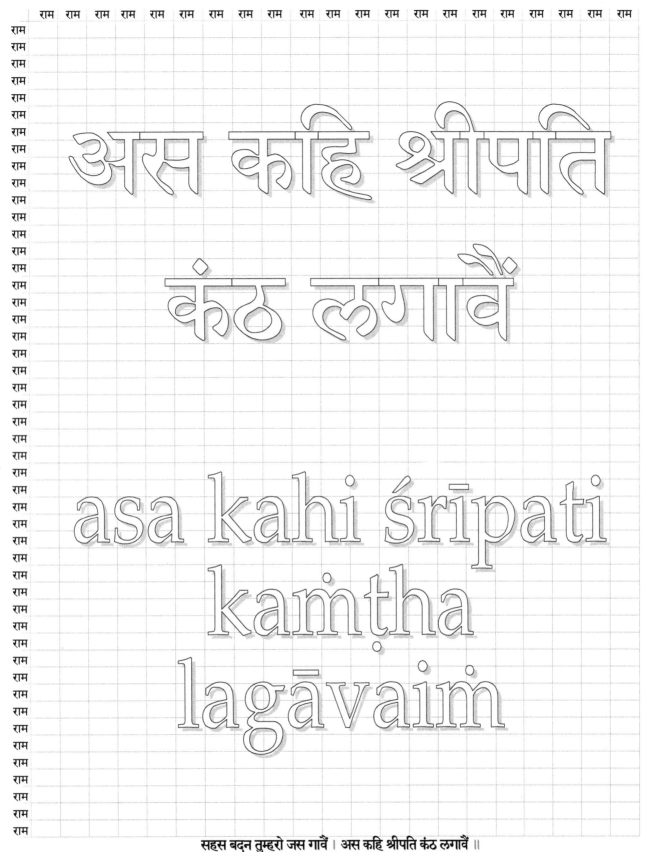

अस कहि श्रीपति

कंठ लगावैं

asa kahi śrīpati
kaṁṭha
lagāvaiṁ

सहस बदन तुम्हरो जस गावैं ॥ अस कहि श्रीपति कंठ लगावैं ॥

sahasa badana tumharo jasa gāvaiṁ, asa kahi śrīpati kaṁṭha lagāvaiṁ. 13.

Thousands of beings are singing your praise—with those words to you, Rāma again to you, unto His heart did raise.

सनकादिक

ब्रह्मादि मुनीशा

sanak-ādika

brahmādi

muniśā

राम
राम
राम
राम
राम
राम
राम
राम
राम
राम
राम
राम
राम
राम
राम
राम
राम
राम
राम
राम
राम
राम
राम
राम
राम
राम
राम
राम
राम
राम
राम
राम
राम
राम
राम

: Today's Date :

राम राम

सनकादिक ब्रह्मादि मुनीशा । नारद शारद सहित अहीशा ॥

sanak-ādika brahmādi munīśā, nārada śārada sahita ahīśā. 14.

Celibate *Rishis* like Sanaka; gods like Brahmmā; the foremost *Munis*; Nārad, Saraswatī with Shiva and Vishnu;

जम कुबेर

दिगपाल जहाँ ते

jama kubera

digapāla

jahāṁ te

राम
राम
राम
राम
राम
राम
राम
राम
राम
राम
राम
राम
राम
राम
राम
राम
राम
राम
राम
राम
राम
राम
राम
राम
राम
राम
राम
राम
राम
राम
राम
राम
राम

राम
राम
राम
राम
राम
राम
राम
राम
राम
राम
राम
राम
राम
राम
राम
राम
राम
राम
राम
राम
राम
राम
राम
राम
राम
राम
राम
राम
राम
राम
राम
राम
राम
राम
राम

कवि कोबिद कहि
सकै कहाँ ते

kabi kobida
kahi sakai
kahāṁ te

जम कुबेर दिगपाल जहाँ ते । कबि कोबिद कहि सकै कहाँ ते ॥

jama kubera digapāla jahāṁ te, kabi kobida kahi sakai kahāṁ te. 15.

the eight *Dikpālas* including Yama and Kubera—they all tell you glory but fail to fully delineate it; how then can mere mortals, poets and Vedic scholars sing your laurels?

तुम उपकार
सुग्रीवहिं कीन्हा

tuma
upakāra
sugrīvahiṁ
kīnhā

राम
राम
राम
राम
राम
राम
राम
राम
राम
राम
राम
राम
राम
राम
राम
राम
राम
राम
राम
राम
राम
राम
राम
राम
राम
राम
राम
राम
राम
राम
राम
राम
राम
राम
राम
राम
राम

: Today's Date :

राम मिलाय

राज पद दीन्हा

rāma milāya

rāja pada

dīnhā

तुम उपकार सुग्रीवहिं कीन्हा । राम मिलाय राज पद दीन्हा ॥

tuma upakāra sugrīvahiṁ kīnhā, rāma milāya rāja pada dīnhā. 16.

You bestowed favor upon Sugrīva—you brought him near to Rāma and made him the King of Kishkindhā.

तुम्हरो मंत्र

विभीषन माना

tumharo

maṁtra

bibhīṣaṇa

mānā

राम
राम
राम
राम
राम
राम
राम
राम
राम
राम
राम
राम
राम
राम
राम
राम
राम
राम
राम
राम
राम
राम
राम
राम
राम
राम
राम
राम
राम
राम
राम
राम
राम
राम
राम
राम
राम
राम
राम

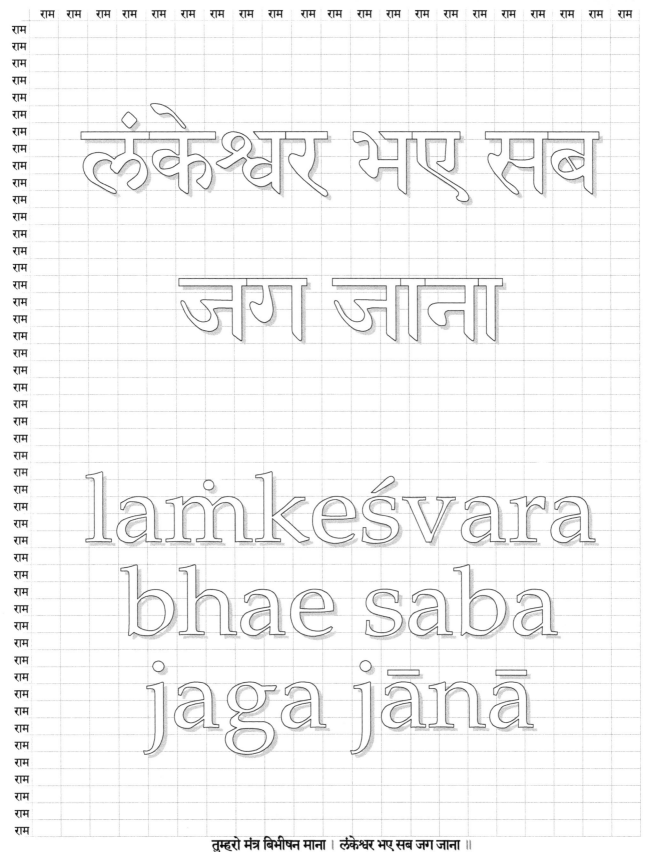

तुम्हरो मंत्र बिभीषन माना । लंकेश्वर भए सब जग जाना ॥

tumharo maṁtra bibhīṣana mānā, laṁkeśvara bhae saba jaga jānā. 17.

Vibhīshan accepted your Mantra, and as consequence became the King of Lankā—this is well known throughout the world.

जुग सहस्त्र

जोजन पर भानू

juga sahastra
jojana para
bhānū

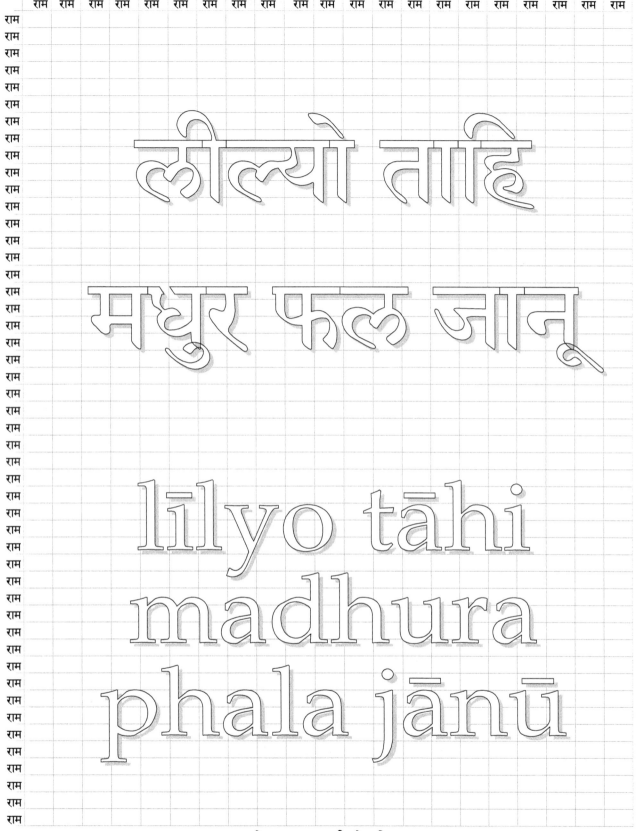

जुग सहस्र जोजन पर भानु । लील्यो ताहि मधुर फल जानू ॥
juga sahastra jojana para bhānū, līlyo tāhi madhura phala jānū. 18.
At a thousand *Yuga Yojan* is the Sun, and mistaking it for a sweet fruit, you supped it up—while still an infant.

प्रभु मुद्रिका

मेलि मुख माहीं

prabhu mudrikā
meli mukha
māhiṁ

राम
राम
राम
राम
राम
राम
राम
राम
राम
राम
राम
राम
राम
राम
राम
राम
राम
राम
राम
राम
राम
राम
राम
राम
राम
राम
राम
राम
राम
राम
राम
राम
राम
राम
राम
राम
राम
राम
राम

: Today's Date :

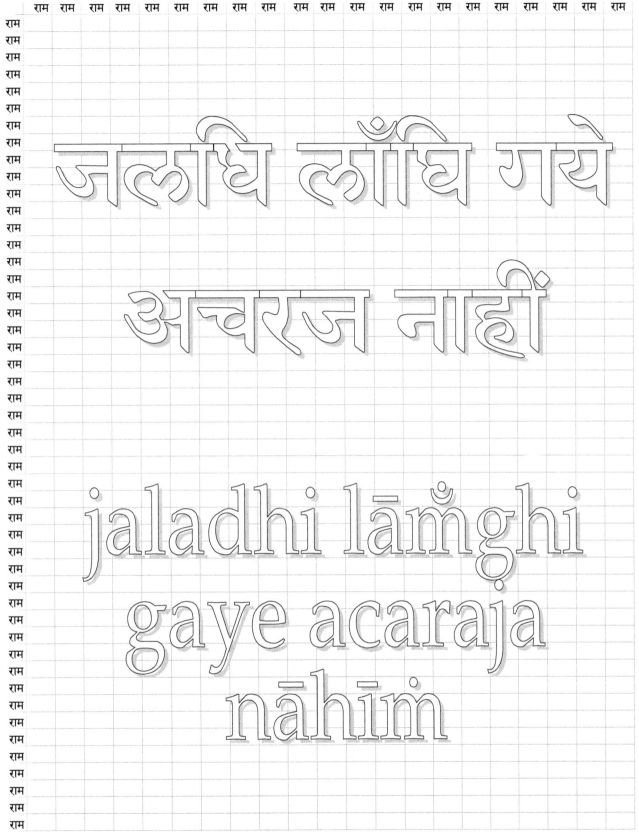

राम
राम
राम
राम
राम
राम
राम
राम
राम
राम
राम
राम
राम
राम
राम
राम
राम
राम
राम
राम
राम
राम
राम
राम
राम
राम
राम
राम
राम
राम
राम
राम
राम
राम
राम
राम
राम
राम
राम
राम

जलधि लाँघि गये

अचरज नाहीं

jaladhi lāṁ̐ghi

gaye acaraja

nāhīṁ

प्रभु मुद्रिका मेलि मुख माहीं । जलधि लाँघि गये अचरज नाहीं ॥

prabhu mudrikā meli mukha māhīṁ, jaladhi lāṁ̐ghi gaye acaraja nāhīṁ. 19.

The ring of the Lord you placed in your mouth and then leaped across the ocean to give it to Sītā. But what wonder is there in that? [Verily, scaling the impossible comes to you with ease.]

दुर्गम काज

जगत के जेते

durgama
kāja jagata ke
jete

राम
राम
राम
राम
राम
राम
राम
राम
राम
राम
राम
राम
राम
राम
राम
राम
राम
राम
राम
राम
राम
राम
राम
राम
राम
राम
राम
राम
राम
राम
राम
राम
राम
राम
राम
राम
राम
राम

सुगम अनुग्रह तुम्हरे तेते

sugama anugraha tumhare tete

दुर्गम काज जगत के जेते । सुगम अनुग्रह तुम्हरे तेते ॥
durgama kāja jagata ke jete, sugama anugraha tumhare tete. 20.
All the difficult tasks of the world become easy were it your pleasure—if there, O Lord, be the favor of
your grace.

राम दुआरे

तुम रखवारे

rāma duāre

tuma

rakhavāre

राम
राम
राम
राम
राम
राम
राम
राम
राम
राम
राम
राम
राम
राम
राम
राम
राम
राम
राम
राम
राम
राम
राम
राम
राम
राम
राम
राम
राम
राम
राम
राम
राम
राम
राम
राम
राम
राम
राम
राम
राम
राम
राम
राम

राम
राम
राम
राम
राम
राम
राम
राम
राम
राम
राम
राम
राम
राम
राम
राम
राम
राम
राम
राम
राम
राम
राम
राम
राम
राम
राम
राम
राम
राम
राम
राम
राम
राम
राम
राम
राम

राम दुआरे तुम रखवारे । होत न आज्ञा बिनु पैसारे ॥
rāma duāre tuma rakhavāre, hota na ājñā binu paisāre. 21.
You are the keeper and protector of doorway to Rāma; without your command, nobody can enter the abode of Shrī Rāma.

सब सुख लहैं

तुम्हारी शरना

saba sukha
lahaiṁ
tumhārī
śaranā

: Today's Date :

राम
राम
राम
राम
राम
राम
राम
राम
राम
राम
राम
राम
राम
राम
राम
राम
राम
राम
राम
राम
राम
राम
राम
राम
राम
राम
राम
राम
राम
राम
राम
राम

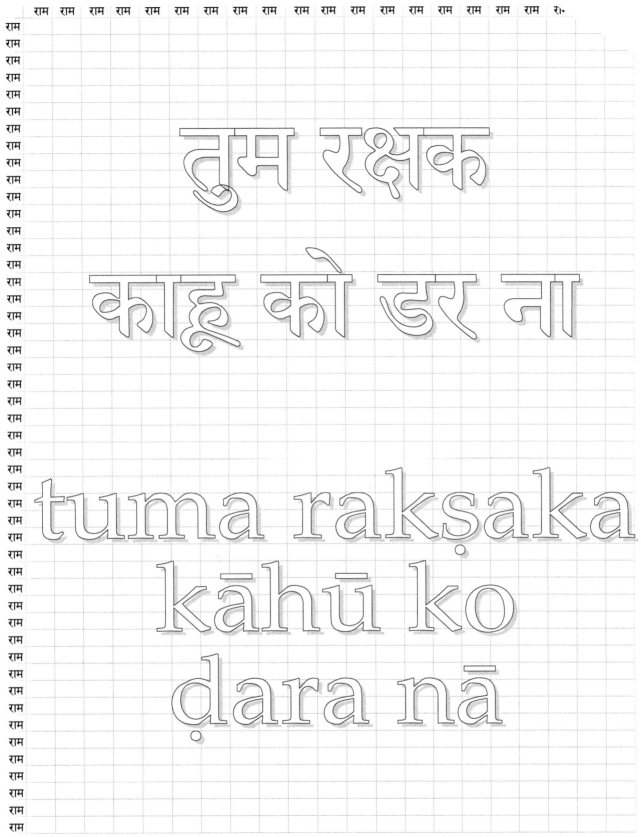

सब सुख लहैं तुम्हारी शरना । तुम रक्षक काहू को डर ना ॥

saba sukha lahaiṁ tumhārī śaranā, tuma rakṣaka kāhū ko ḍara nā. 22.

Every happiness abides with those who bide under your protection. With you as one's guardian, there is never any cause of fear.

आपन तेज

सम्हारो आपै

āpana teja
samhāro āpai

राम
राम
राम
राम
राम
राम
राम
राम
राम
राम
राम
राम
राम
राम
राम
राम
राम
राम
राम
राम
राम
राम
राम
राम
राम
राम
राम
राम
राम
राम
राम
राम
राम
राम
राम
राम
राम
राम
राम

तीनौं लोक

हाँक ते काँपै

tīnauṁ loka
hāṁ̐ka te
kāṁ̐pai

आपन तेज सम्हारो आपै । तीनौं लोक हाँक ते काँपै ॥
āpana teja samhāro āpai, tīnauṁ loka hāṁ̐ka te kāṁ̐pai. 23.
You alone can withstand your own splendor; verily the three worlds quake when your thunder.

भूत पिशाच

निकट नहिं आवै

bhūta piśāca
nikaṭa nahiṃ
āvai

राम
राम
राम
राम
राम
राम
राम
राम
राम
राम
राम
राम
राम
राम
राम
राम
राम
राम
राम
राम
राम
राम
राम
राम
राम
राम
राम
राम
राम
राम
राम
राम
राम
राम
राम
राम
राम
राम
राम

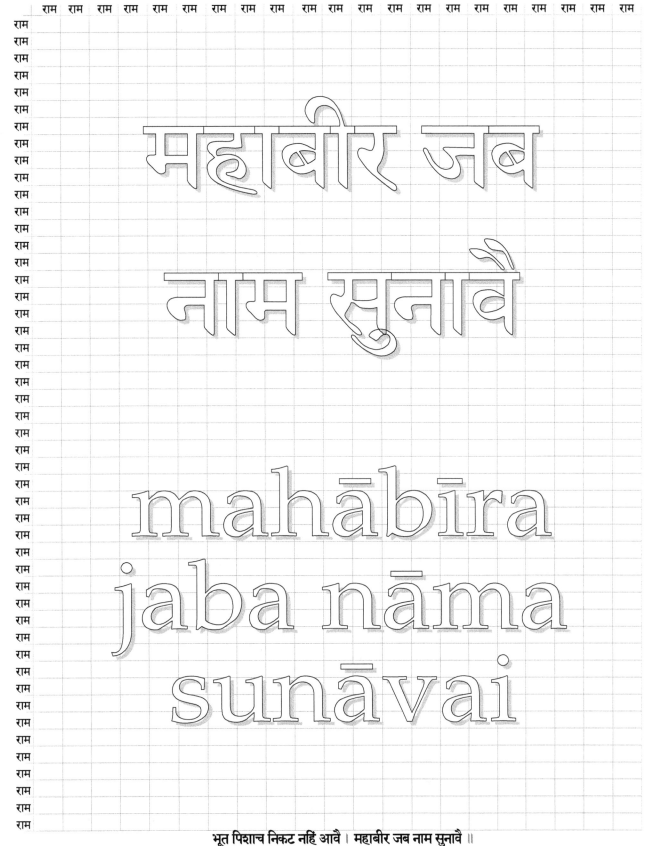

भूत पिशाच निकट नहिं आवै । महाबीर जब नाम सुनावै ॥

bhūta piśāca nikaṭa nahiṁ āvai, mahābīra jaba nāma sunāvai. 24.

Evil spirits and ghosts dare come near not: when the chant of Mahābīra—your name—is invoked.

नासै रोग

हरै सब पीरा

nāsai roga
harai saba
pīrā

राम
राम
राम
राम
राम
राम
राम
राम
राम
राम
राम
राम
राम
राम
राम
राम
राम
राम
राम
राम
राम
राम
राम
राम
राम
राम
राम
राम
राम
राम
राम
राम
राम
राम
राम
राम
राम
राम

राम
राम
राम
राम
राम
राम
राम
राम
राम
राम
राम
राम
राम
राम
राम
राम
राम
राम
राम
राम
राम
राम
राम
राम
राम
राम
राम
राम
राम
राम
राम
राम
राम
राम
राम
राम

नासै रोग हरै सब पीरा । जपत निरंतर हनुमत बीरा ॥

nāsai roga harai saba pīrā, japata niraṁtara hanumata bīrā. 25.

All diseases are destroyed, all pains are ended—with the constant chant of the Name 'Hanumān', the Brave-Supreme.

संकट ते

हनुमान छुड़ावै

saṁkaṭa te

hanumāna

churāvai

राम
राम
राम
राम
राम
राम
राम
राम
राम
राम
राम
राम
राम
राम
राम
राम
राम
राम
राम
राम
राम
राम
राम
राम
राम
राम
राम
राम
राम
राम
राम
राम
राम
राम
राम
राम
राम
राम
राम

: Today's Date :

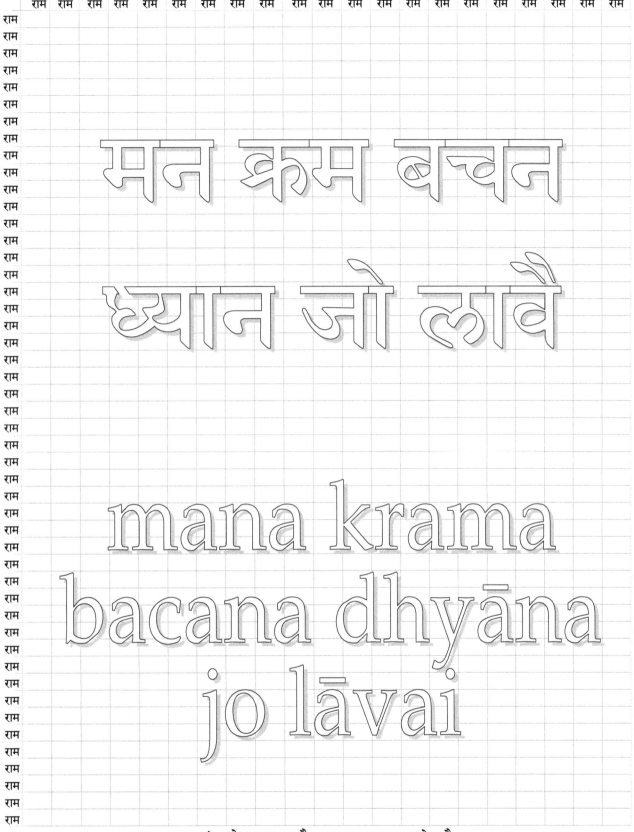

मन क्रम बचन ध्यान जो लावै

मन क्रम बचन ध्यान जो लावै

mana krama bacana dhyāna jo lāvai

संकट ते हनुमान छुड़ावै । मन क्रम बचन ध्यान जो लावै ॥

saṁkaṭa te hanumāna chuṛāvai, mana krama bacana dhyāna jo lāvai. 26.

Lord Hanumān removes all afflictions, every adversity—for those who remember him in heart, word & deed.

सब पर राम

तपस्वी राजा

saba para
rāma tapasvī
rājā

राम
राम
राम
राम
राम
राम
राम
राम
राम
राम
राम
राम
राम
राम
राम
राम
राम
राम
राम
राम
राम
राम
राम
राम
राम
राम
राम
राम
राम
राम
राम
राम
राम
राम
राम
राम
राम

सब पर राम तपस्वी राजा । तिन के काज सकल तुम साजा ॥
saba para rāma tapasvī rājā, tina ke kāja sakala tuma sājā. 27.
Rāma, the Ascetic-King, is the sovereign ruler over all; and it is you who administer his works.

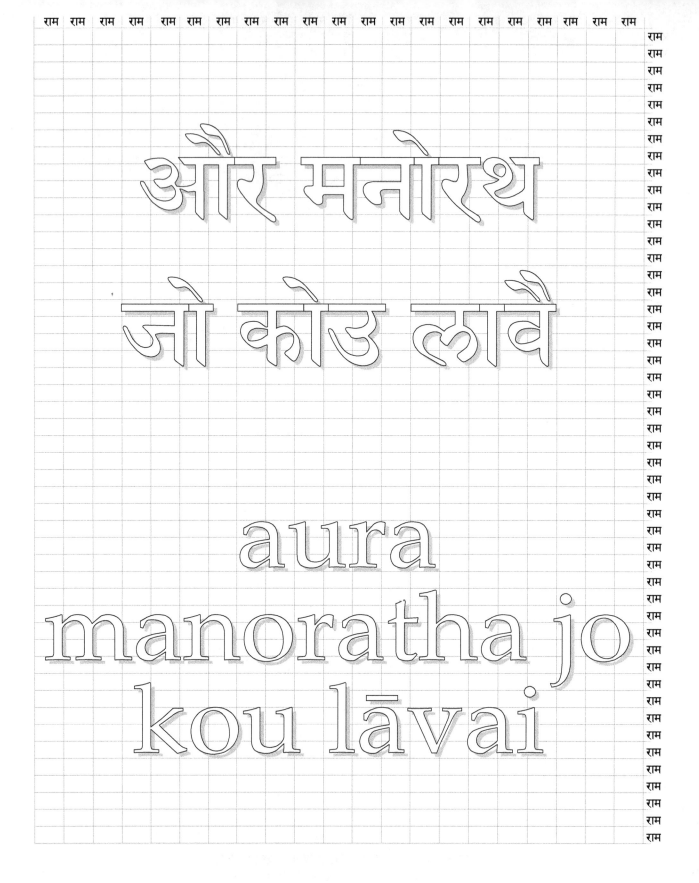

और मनोरथ

जो कोउ लावै

aura
manoratha jo
kou lāvai

राम
राम
राम
राम
राम
राम
राम
राम
राम
राम
राम
राम
राम
राम
राम
राम
राम
राम
राम
राम
राम
राम
राम
राम
राम
राम
राम
राम
राम
राम
राम
राम
राम
राम
राम
राम
राम
राम

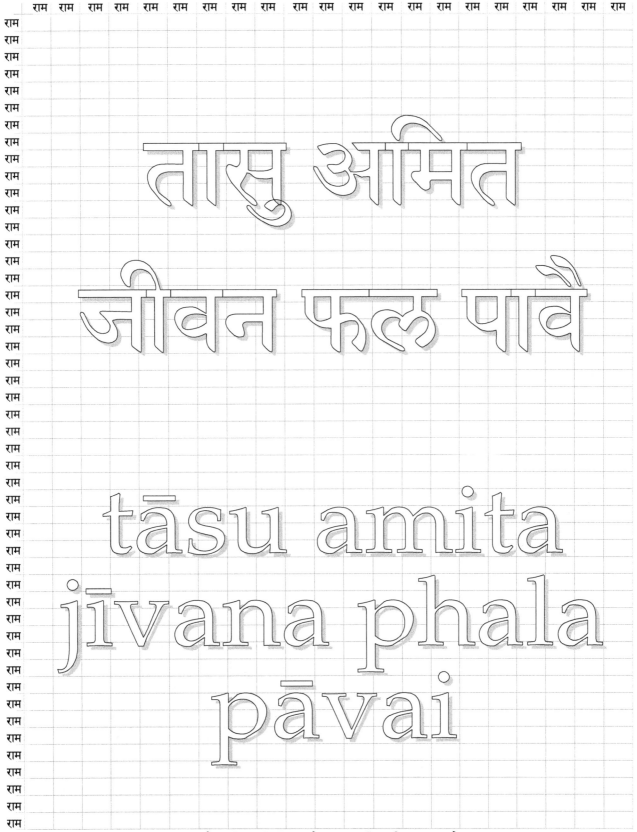

तासु अमित

जीवन फल पावै

tāsu amita

jīvana phala

pāvai

और मनोरथ जो कोउ लावै । तासु अमित जीवन फल पावै ॥

aura manoratha jo kou lāvai, tāsu amita jīvana phala pāvai. 28.

When one comes to you with a heart's desire, you yield unto him unlimited fruits for the whole life in entire.

चारों जुग

परताप तुम्हारा

cāroṁ juga
paratāpa
tumhārā

राम
राम
राम
राम
राम
राम
राम
राम
राम
राम
राम
राम
राम
राम
राम
राम
राम
राम
राम
राम
राम
राम
राम
राम
राम
राम
राम
राम
राम
राम
राम
राम
राम

: Today's Date :

राम
राम
राम
राम
राम
राम
राम
राम
राम
राम
राम
राम
राम
राम
राम
राम
राम
राम
राम
राम
राम
राम
राम
राम
राम
राम
राम
राम
राम
राम
राम

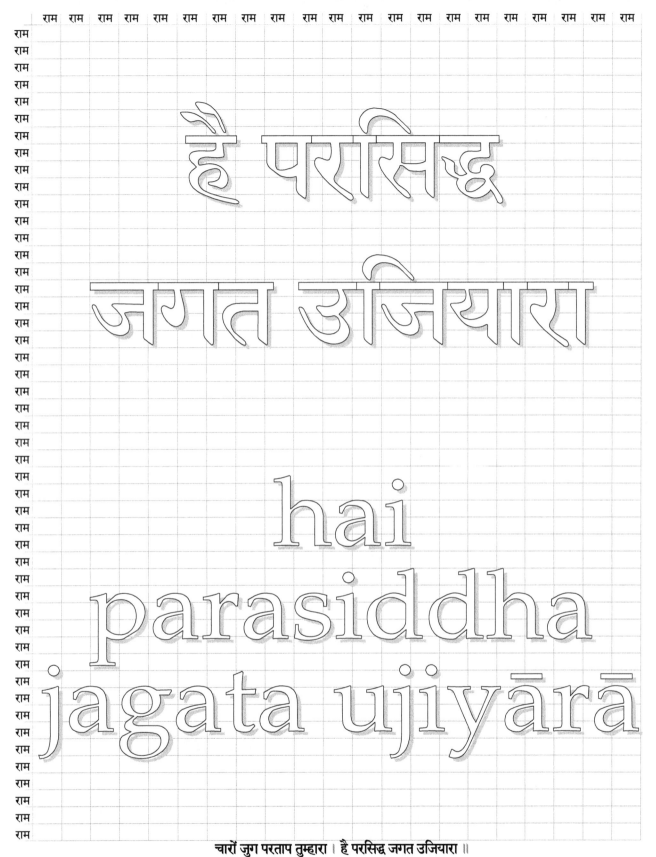

है परसिद्ध

जगत उजियारा

hai
parasiddha
jagata ujiyārā

चारों जुग परताप तुम्हारा । है परसिद्ध जगत उजियारा ॥

cāroṁ juga paratāpa tumhārā, hai parasiddha jagata ujiyārā. 29.

Your resplendency persists across all the times; in all the four *Yugas*, your fame illumines throughout the universe.

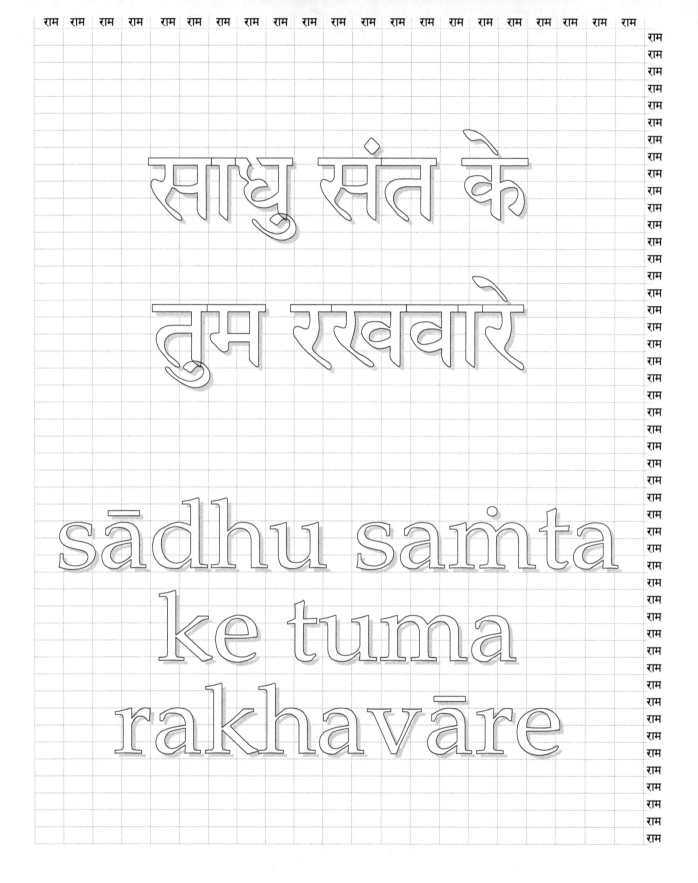

साधु संत के

तुम रखवारे

sādhu saṁta

ke tuma

rakhavāre

राम
राम
राम
राम
राम
राम
राम
राम
राम
राम
राम
राम
राम
राम
राम
राम
राम
राम
राम
राम
राम
राम
राम
राम
राम
राम
राम
राम
राम
राम
राम
राम
राम
राम
राम
राम
राम

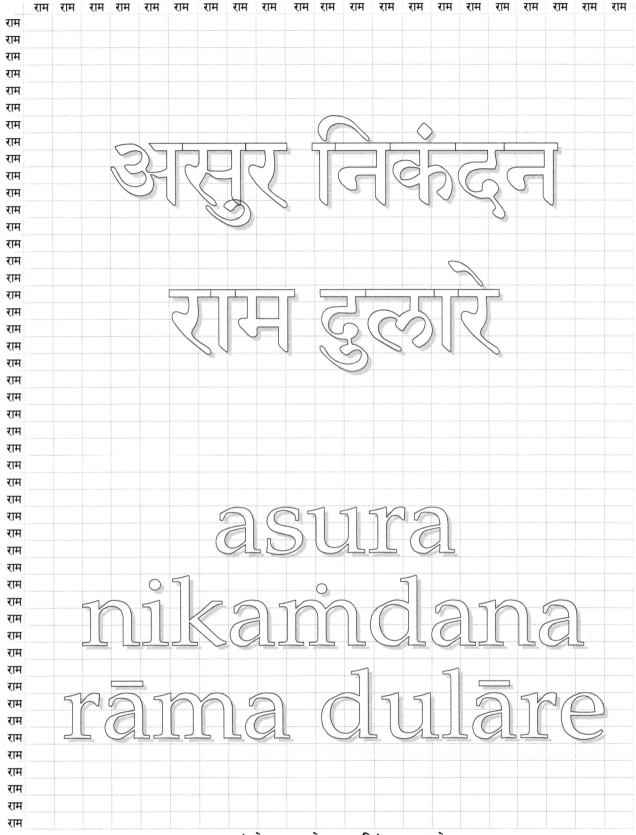

साधु संत के तुम रखवारे । **असुर निकंदन राम दुलारे** ॥

sādhu saṁta ke tuma rakhavāre, asura nikaṁdana rāma dulāre. 30.

You—dear-most son of Rāma—are the guardian of the saintly, virtuous, wise; and you are the destroyer of the fiends and the vile.

अष्ट सिद्धि नव
निधि के दाता

aṣṭa siddhi
nava nidhi
ke dātā

राम
राम
राम
राम
राम
राम
राम
राम
राम
राम
राम
राम
राम
राम
राम
राम
राम
राम
राम
राम
राम
राम
राम
राम
राम
राम
राम
राम
राम
राम
राम
राम
राम
राम
राम
राम
राम

: Today's Date :

अष्ट सिद्धि नव निधि के दाता । अस बर दीन्ह जानकी माता ॥
aṣṭa siddhi nava nidhi ke dātā, asa bara dīnha jānakī mātā. 31.
You are the bestower of all eight *Siddhis* and nine *Nidhis*—Mother Sītā, daughter of Janak, herself
endowed you with that power.

राम रसायन

तुम्हरे पासा

rāma

rasāyana

tumhare

pāsā

राम
राम
राम
राम
राम
राम
राम
राम
राम
राम
राम
राम
राम
राम
राम
राम
राम
राम
राम
राम
राम
राम
राम
राम
राम
राम
राम
राम
राम
राम
राम
राम
राम
राम
राम
राम
राम
राम
राम

: Today's Date :

सदा रहउ

रघुपति के दासा

sadā rahau
raghupati ke
dāsā

राम रसायन तुम्हरे पासा ꠰ सदा रहउ रघुपति के दासा ꠰꠰

rāma rasāyana tumhare pāsā, sadā rahau raghupati ke dāsā. 32.

You own the sweet treasure of devotion to Rāma; you ever abide as the foremost attendant of that Jewel of Rhagu scion.

तुम्हरे भजन

राम को पावै

tumhare
bhajana rāma ko
pāvai

राम
राम
राम
राम
राम
राम
राम
राम
राम
राम
राम
राम
राम
राम
राम
राम
राम
राम
राम
राम
राम
राम
राम
राम
राम
राम
राम
राम
राम
राम
राम
राम
राम
राम

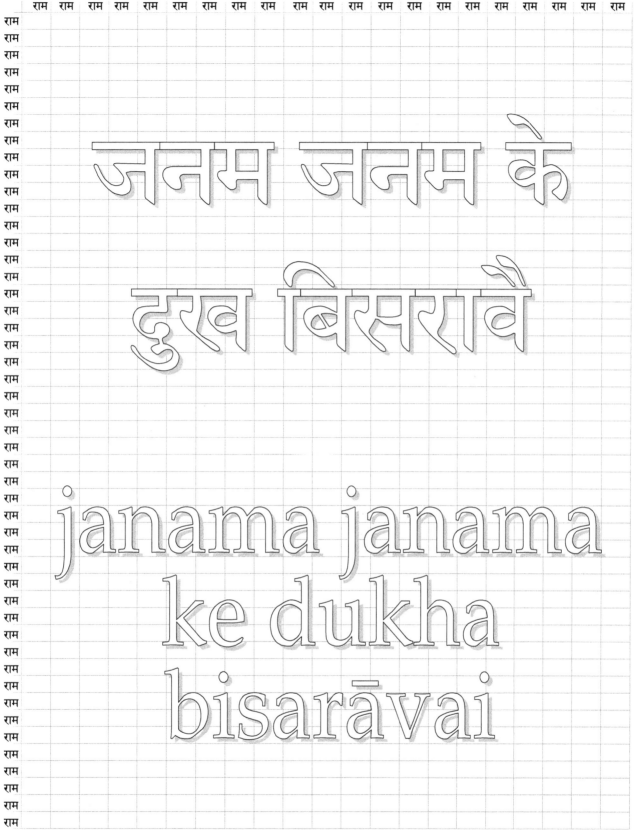

तुम्हरे भजन राम को पावै । जनम जनम के दुख बिसरावै ॥

tumhare bhajana rāma ko pāvai, janama janama ke dukha bisarāvai. 33.

Through devotion to you one is able to obtain to the Lord; and the adversities and afflictions of millions of births become defeated thereupon;

अंत काळ

रघुबर पुर जाई

amta kāla

raghubara

pura jāī

राम
राम
राम
राम
राम
राम
राम
राम
राम
राम
राम
राम
राम
राम
राम
राम
राम
राम
राम
राम
राम
राम
राम
राम
राम
राम
राम
राम
राम
राम
राम
राम
राम
राम
राम
राम
राम
राम
राम

: Today's Date :

राम
राम
राम
राम
राम
राम
राम
राम
राम
राम
राम
राम
राम
राम
राम
राम
राम
राम
राम
राम
राम
राम
राम
राम
राम
राम
राम
राम
राम
राम
राम
राम
राम

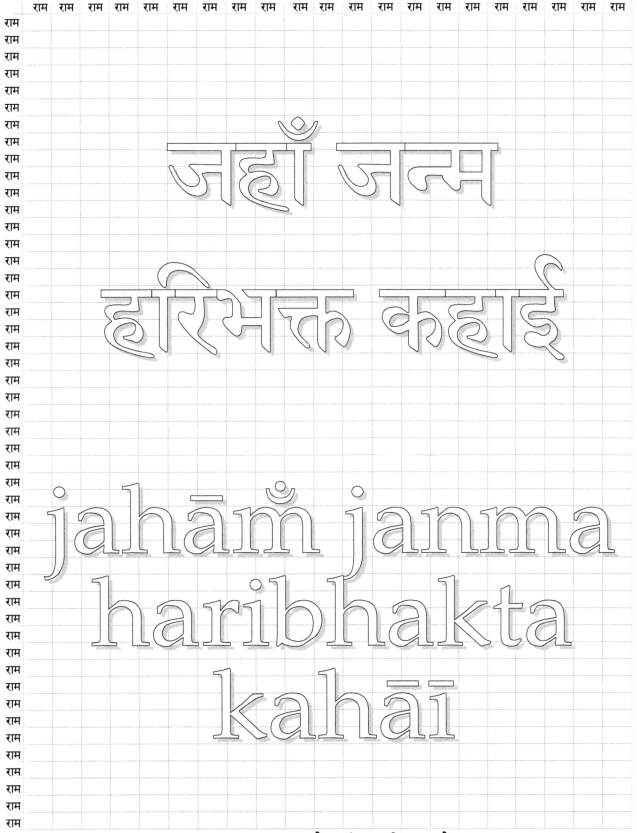

जहाँ जन्म हरिभक्त कहाई

jahāṁ janma haribhakta kahāī

अंत काल रघुबर पुर जाई । जहाँ जन्म हरिभक्त कहाई ॥

aṁta kāla raghubara pura jāī, jahāṁ janma haribhakta kahāī. 34.

and at the time of their end, one goes to Rāma's own abode—remaining there eternally as Rāma's very own.

और देवता

चित्त न धरई

aura devatā
citta na
dharai

: Today's Date :

राम
राम
राम
राम
राम
राम
राम
राम
राम
राम
राम
राम
राम
राम
राम
राम
राम
राम
राम
राम
राम
राम
राम
राम
राम
राम
राम
राम
राम
राम
राम
राम
राम
राम
राम
राम

हनुमत सेइ

सर्ब सुख करई

hanumata sei

sarba sukha

karaī

और देवता चित्त न धरई । हनुमत सेइ सर्ब सुख करई ॥

aura devatā citta na dharaī, hanumata sei sarba sukha karaī. 35.

Swearing by no other god, and just serving Shrī Hanumān alone—one obtains every happiness in this world and the next.

संकट कटै
मिटै सब पीरा

samkaṭa
kaṭai miṭai
saba pīrā

राम
राम
राम
राम
राम
राम
राम
राम
राम
राम
राम
राम
राम
राम
राम
राम
राम
राम
राम
राम
राम
राम
राम
राम
राम
राम
राम
राम
राम
राम
राम
राम
राम
राम
राम
राम
राम
राम

: Today's Date :

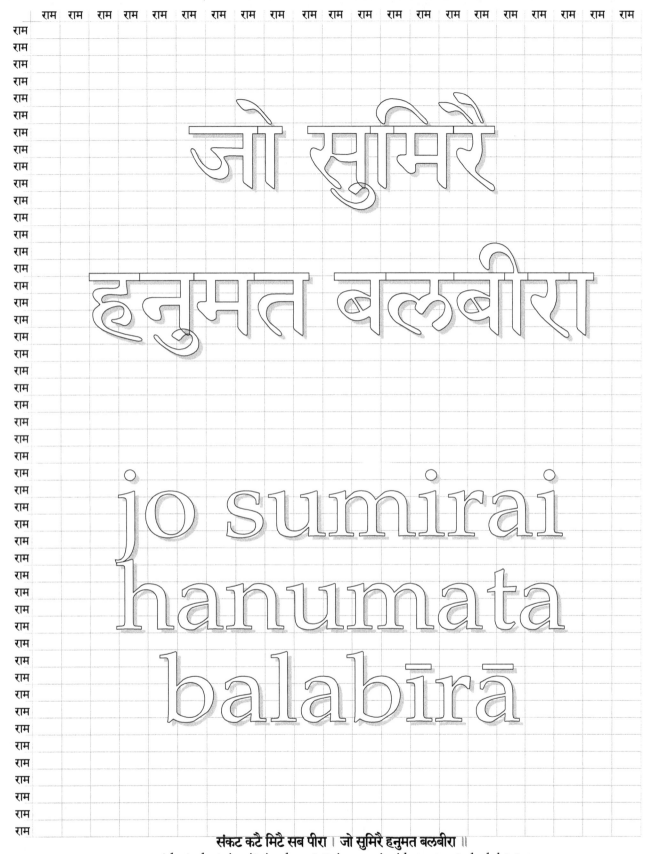

जो सुमिरै

हनुमत बलबीरा

jo sumirai
hanumata
balabīrā

संकट कटै मिटै सब पीरा । जो सुमिरै हनुमत बलबीरा ॥

saṁkaṭa kaṭai miṭai saba pīrā, jo sumirai hanumata balabīrā. 36.

All troubles are cut short, all pains removed—for they who meditate upon Hanumān, the mighty, brave, supreme.

जय जय जय

हनुमान गोसाईं

jaya jaya jaya
hanumāna
gosāiṁ

राम
राम
राम
राम
राम
राम
राम
राम
राम
राम
राम
राम
राम
राम
राम
राम
राम
राम
राम
राम
राम
राम
राम
राम
राम
राम
राम
राम
राम
राम
राम
राम
राम
राम
राम
राम
राम

: Today's Date :

राम
राम
राम
राम
राम
राम
राम
राम
राम
राम
राम
राम
राम
राम
राम
राम
राम
राम
राम
राम
राम
राम
राम
राम
राम
राम
राम
राम
राम
राम

कृपा करहु
गुरु देव की नाईं

kṛpā karahu
guru deva kī
nāīṁ

जय जय जय हनुमान गोसाईं ꠰ कृपा करहु गुरु देव की नाईं ꠰꠰

jaya jaya jaya hanumāna gosāīṁ, kṛpā karahu guru deva kī nāīṁ. 37.

Victory to you Hanumān, O master of senses. May you remain ever victorious, ever triumphant. Shower your grace upon us—as lovingly as a Guru does.

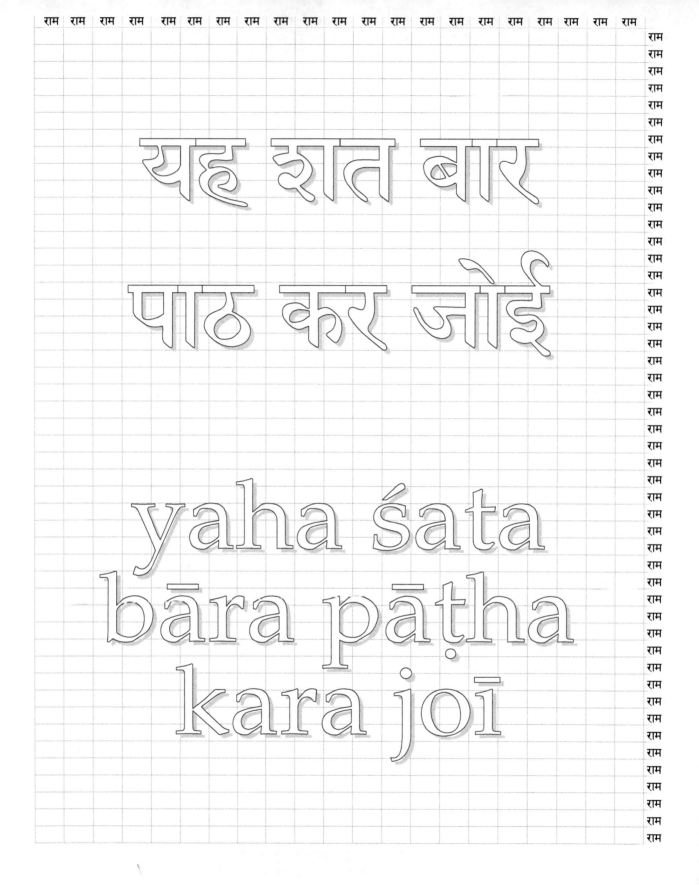

यह शत वार

पाठ कर जोई

yaha śata

bāra pāṭha

kara joī

राम
राम
राम
राम
राम
राम
राम
राम
राम
राम
राम
राम
राम
राम
राम
राम
राम
राम
राम
राम
राम
राम
राम
राम
राम
राम
राम
राम
राम
राम
राम
राम
राम
राम
राम
राम

: Today's Date :

राम
राम
राम
राम
राम
राम
राम
राम
राम
राम
राम
राम
राम
राम
राम
राम
राम
राम
राम
राम
राम
राम
राम
राम
राम
राम
राम
राम
राम
राम

छूटै बंदि महा सुख सोई

chūṭai baṁdi mahā sukha soī

यह शत बार पाठ कर जोई । छूटै बंदि महा सुख सोई ॥

yaha śata bāra pāṭha kara joī, chūṭai baṁdi mahā sukha soī. 38.

One who recites this Hanumān Chālīsā a hundred times is released from all bondages and obtains bliss everlasting.

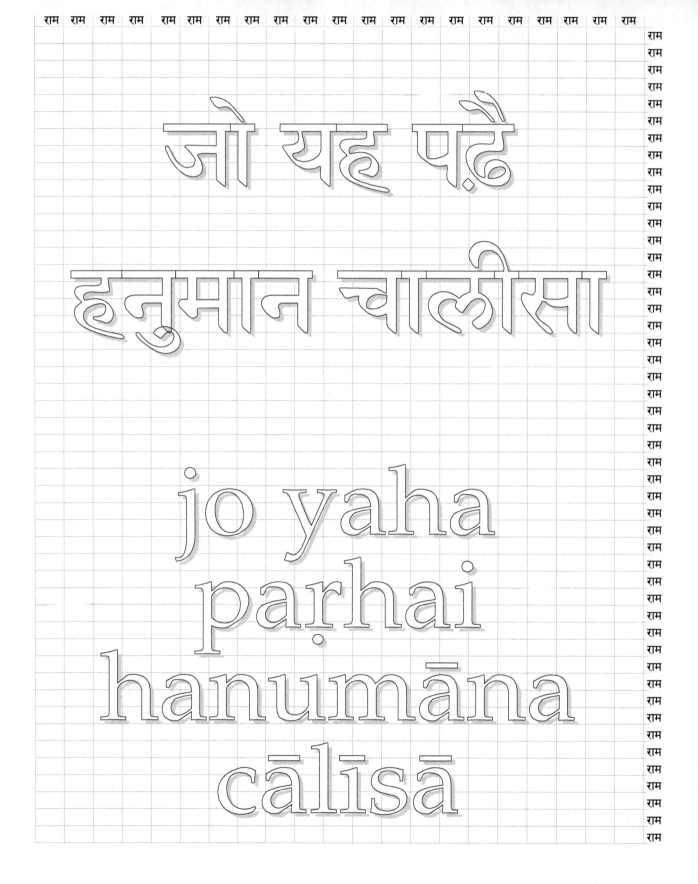

जो यह पढ़ै

हनुमान चालीसा

jo yaha

paṛhai

hanumāna

cālīsā

राम
राम
राम
राम
राम
राम
राम
राम
राम
राम
राम
राम
राम
राम
राम
राम
राम
राम
राम
राम
राम
राम
राम
राम
राम
राम
राम
राम
राम
राम
राम
राम

: Today's Date :

राम
राम
राम
राम
राम
राम
राम
राम
राम
राम
राम
राम
राम
राम
राम
राम
राम
राम
राम
राम
राम
राम
राम
राम
राम
राम
राम
राम
राम
राम
राम
राम
राम
राम
राम
राम

जो यह पढ़ै हनुमान चालीसा । **होय सिद्धि साखी गौरीसा ॥**

jo yaha paṛhai hanumāna cālīsā, hoya siddhi sākhī gaurīsā. 39.

One who reads this Hanumān Chālīsā becomes a *Siddha*—Gaurī's Lord Shiva himself bears witness to that.

तुलसीदास

सदा हरि चेरा

tulasī-dāsa

sadā hari

cerā

राम
राम
राम
राम
राम
राम
राम
राम
राम
राम
राम
राम
राम
राम
राम
राम
राम
राम
राम
राम
राम
राम
राम
राम
राम
राम
राम
राम
राम
राम
राम
राम
राम
राम
राम
राम
राम
राम
राम
राम

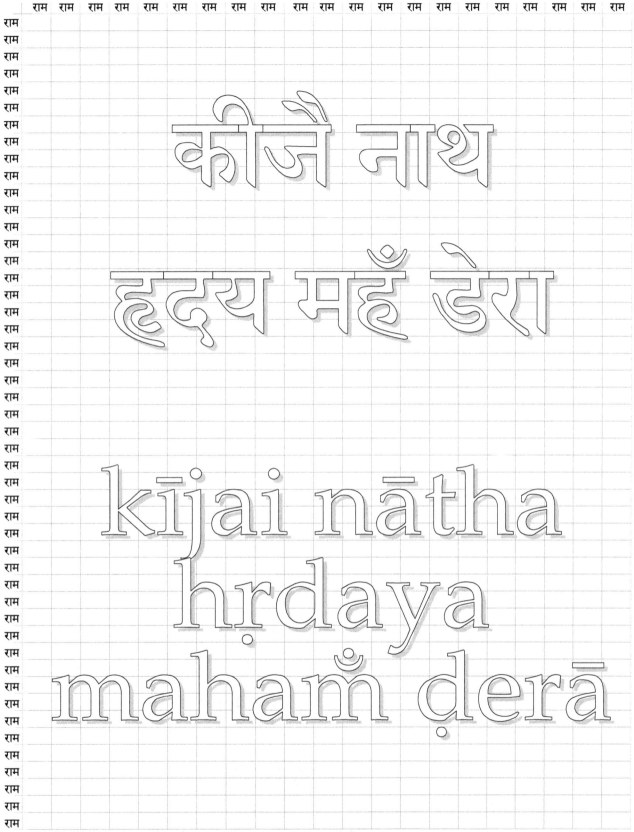

कीजै नाथ

हृदय महँ डेरा

kījai nātha

hṛdaya

mahaṁ ḍerā

तुलसीदास सदा हरि चेरा ꘡ कीजै नाथ हृदय महँ डेरा ॥

tulasī-dāsa sadā hari cerā, kījai nātha hṛdaya mahaṁ ḍerā. 40.

Tulsīdās is ever a disciple of Shrī Rāma; O Lord Hanumān, do please take up thy abode in my heart as well.

पवन तनय

संकट हरन

pavana
tanaya
saṁkaṭa
harana

राम
राम
राम
राम
राम
राम
राम
राम
राम
राम
राम
राम
राम
राम
राम
राम
राम
राम
राम
राम
राम
राम
राम
राम
राम
राम
राम
राम
राम
राम
राम
राम
राम
राम
राम
राम
राम
राम
राम
राम
राम

राम
राम
राम
राम
राम
राम
राम
राम
राम
राम
राम
राम
राम
राम
राम
राम
राम
राम
राम
राम
राम
राम
राम
राम
राम
राम
राम
राम
राम
राम
राम
राम
राम
राम

मंगल मूरति रूप

mamgala mūrati rūpa

दोहा - dohā

पवन तनय संकट हरन मंगल मूरति रूप ।

pavana tanaya saṁkaṭa harana maṁgala mūrati rūpa,

O Son-of-Wind, remover of all disasters & sin—O Radiant-One, of the most auspicious visage—

राम लखन

सीता सहित

rāma
lakhana sītā
sahita

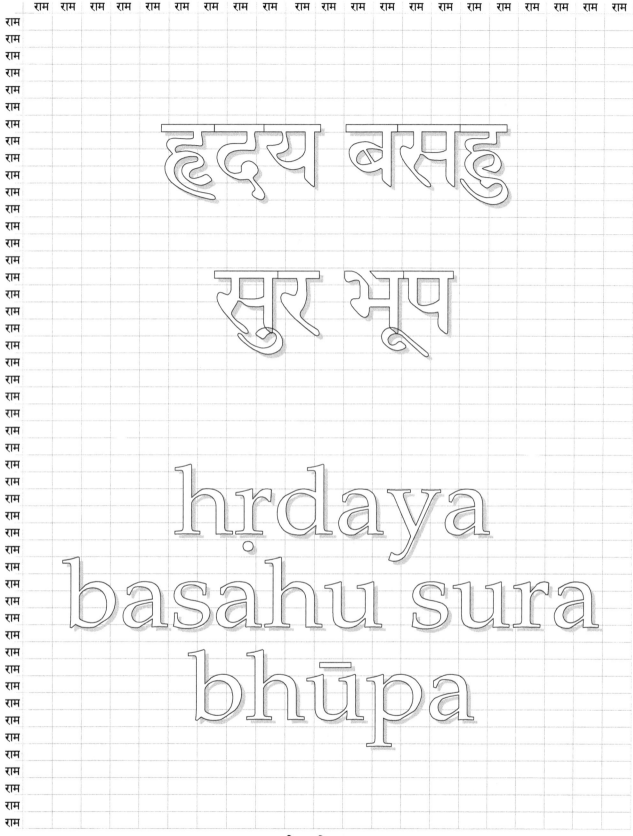

हृदय बसहु

सुर भूप

hṛdaya
basahu sura
bhūpa

राम लखन सीता सहित हृदय बसहु सुर भूप ॥
rāma lakhana sītā sahita hṛdaya basahu sura bhūpa.
may you ever and ever abide within my heart—along with Lakshman, Sītā, Rāma—O first amongst all
gods.

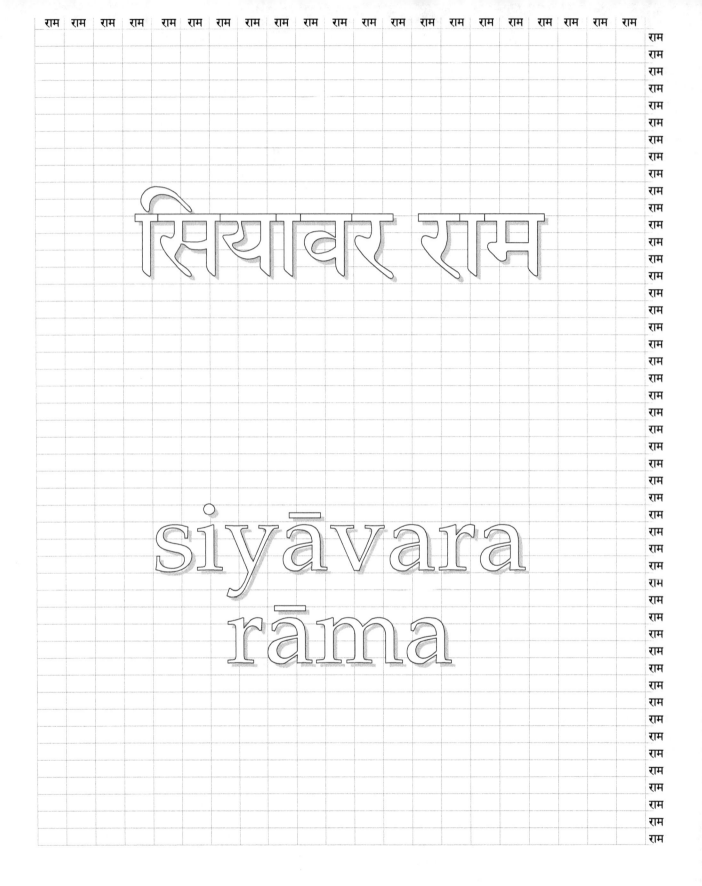

सियावर राम

siyāvara
rāma

राम
राम
राम
राम
राम
राम
राम
राम
राम
राम
राम
राम
राम
राम
राम
राम
राम
राम
राम
राम
राम
राम
राम
राम
राम
राम
राम
राम
राम
राम
राम
राम
राम
राम
राम
राम
राम
राम
राम
राम
राम

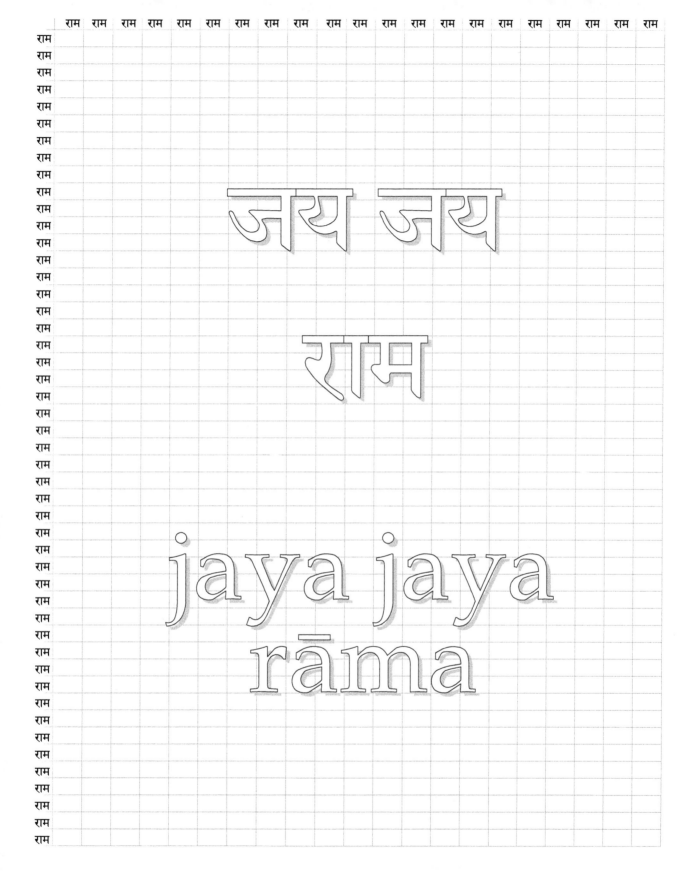

जय जय

राम

jaya jaya
rāma

मेरे प्रभु

राम

mere prabhu
rāma

राम
राम
राम
राम
राम
राम
राम
राम
राम
राम
राम
राम
राम
राम
राम
राम
राम
राम
राम
राम
राम
राम
राम
राम
राम
राम
राम
राम
राम
राम
राम
राम
राम
राम
राम
राम
राम
राम
राम
राम

: Today's Date :

राम राम

राम
राम
राम
राम
राम
राम
राम
राम
राम
राम
राम
राम
राम
राम
राम
राम
राम
राम
राम
राम
राम
राम
राम
राम
राम
राम
राम
राम
राम
राम
राम
राम
राम
राम

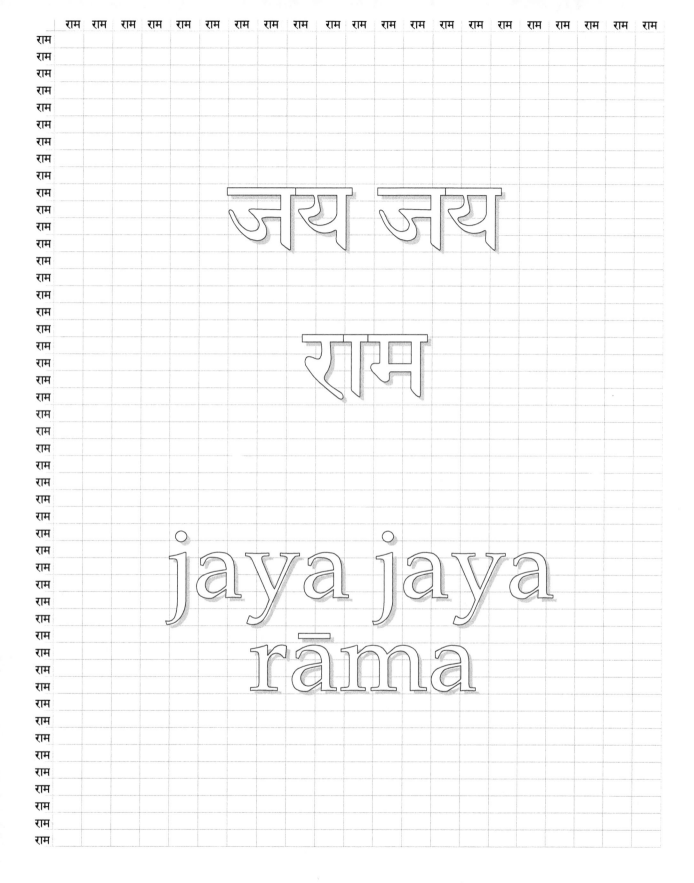

जय जय

राम

jaya jaya

rāma

राम
राम
राम
राम
राम
राम
राम
राम
राम
राम
राम
राम
राम
राम
राम
राम
राम
राम
राम
राम
राम
राम
राम
राम
राम
राम
राम
राम
राम
राम
राम
राम
राम
राम
राम
राम
राम
राम
राम

राम
राम
राम
राम
राम
राम
राम
राम
राम
राम
राम
राम
राम
राम
राम
राम
राम
राम
राम
राम
राम
राम
राम
राम
राम
राम
राम
राम
राम
राम
राम
राम
राम
राम
राम
राम
राम
राम
राम
राम

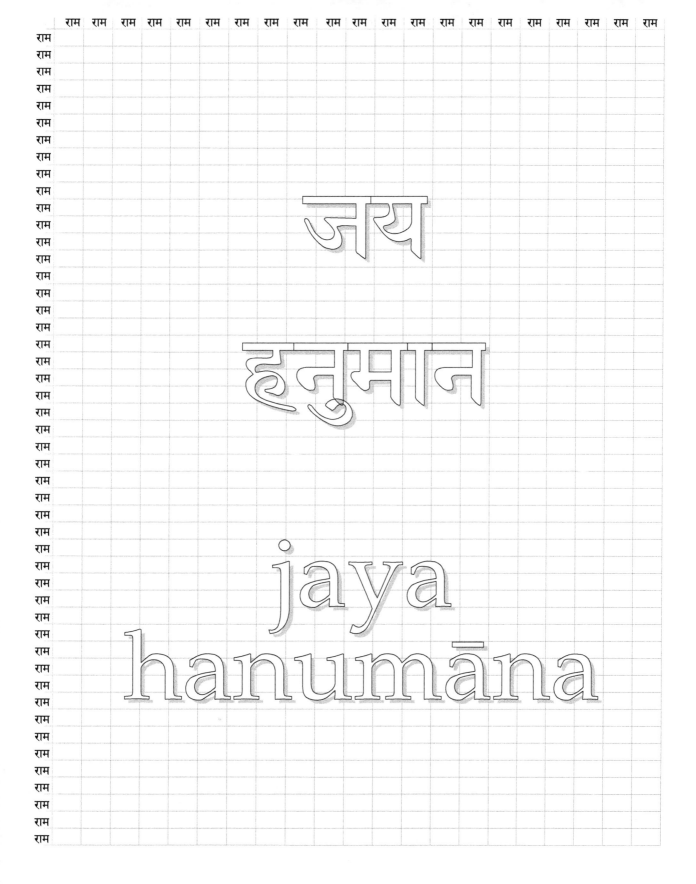

जय

हनुमान

jaya
hanumāna

सीताराम

sitārāma

राम
राम
राम
राम
राम
राम
राम
राम
राम
राम
राम
राम
राम
राम
राम
राम
राम
राम
राम
राम
राम
राम
राम
राम
राम
राम
राम
राम
राम
राम
राम
राम
राम
राम
राम
राम
राम
राम
राम
राम
राम
राम
राम

Today's Date :

राम
राम
राम
राम
राम
राम
राम
राम
राम
राम
राम
राम
राम
राम
राम
राम
राम
राम
राम
राम
राम
राम
राम
राम
राम
राम
राम
राम
राम
राम
राम
राम
राम
राम
राम
राम
राम
राम

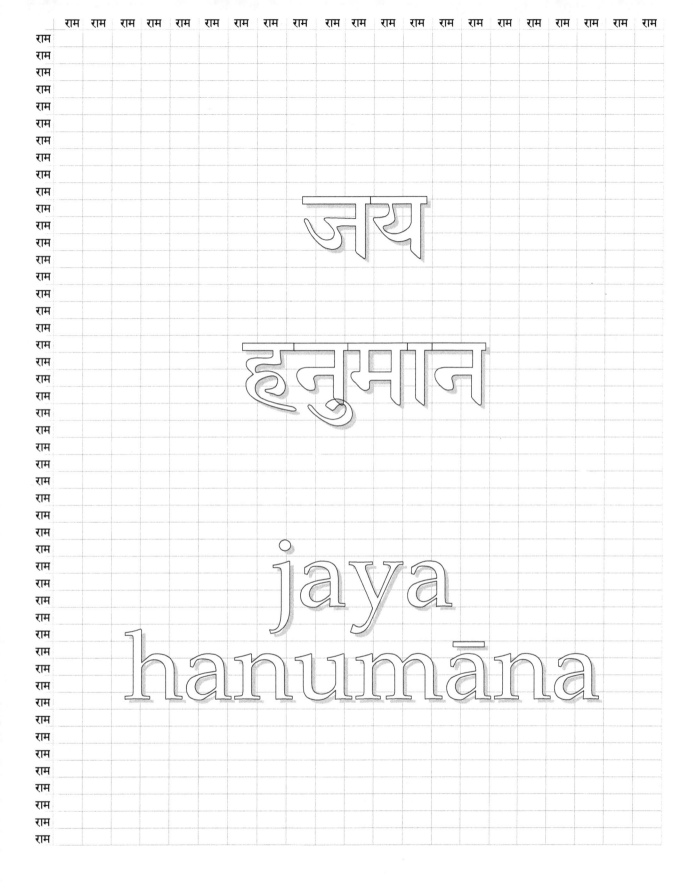

जय

हनुमान

jaya
hanumāna

सीताराम

sītārāma

राम
राम
राम
राम
राम
राम
राम
राम
राम
राम
राम
राम
राम
राम
राम
राम
राम
राम
राम
राम
राम
राम
राम
राम
राम
राम
राम
राम
राम
राम
राम
राम
राम
राम
राम
राम
राम
राम
राम

Today's Date :

राम
राम
राम
राम
राम
राम
राम
राम
राम
राम
राम
राम
राम
राम
राम
राम
राम
राम
राम
राम
राम
राम
राम
राम
राम
राम
राम
राम
राम
राम
राम
राम
राम
राम
राम
राम
राम

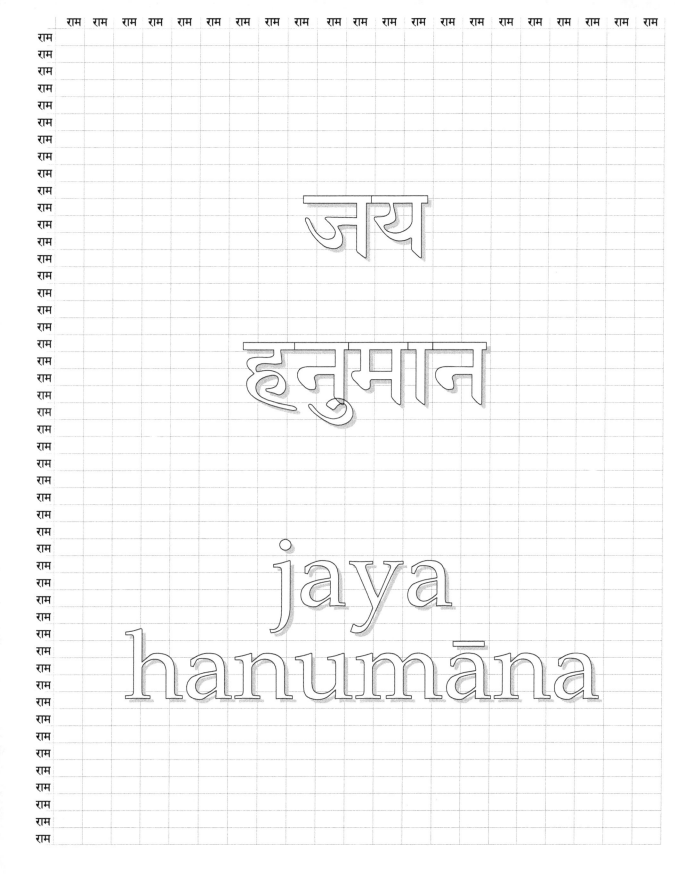

जय

हनुमान

jaya
hanumāna

सीताराम

sītārāma

: Today's Date :

राम
राम
राम
राम
राम
राम
राम
राम
राम
राम
राम
राम
राम
राम
राम
राम
राम
राम
राम
राम
राम
राम
राम
राम
राम
राम
राम
राम
राम
राम
राम
राम
राम
राम
राम
राम
राम
राम
राम

राम
राम
राम
राम
राम
राम
राम
राम
राम
राम
राम
राम
राम
राम
राम
राम
राम
राम
राम
राम
राम
राम
राम
राम
राम
राम
राम
राम
राम
राम
राम
राम
राम
राम
राम
राम
राम
राम

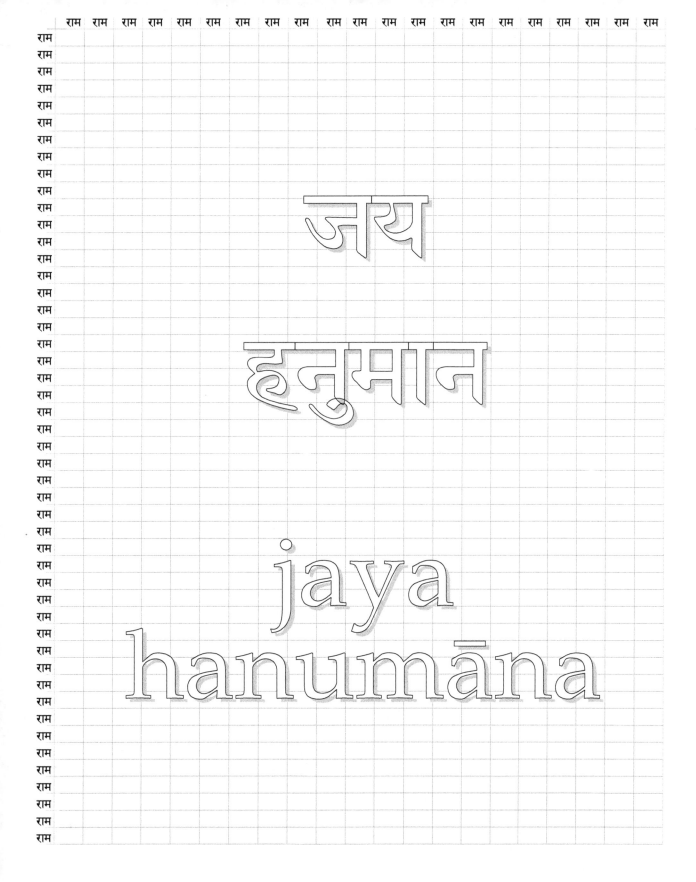

जय

हनुमान

jaya
hanumāna

सीताराम

sitārāma

राम
राम
राम
राम
राम
राम
राम
राम
राम
राम
राम
राम
राम
राम
राम
राम
राम
राम
राम
राम
राम
राम
राम
राम
राम
राम
राम
राम
राम
राम
राम
राम
राम
राम
राम
राम
राम
राम
राम
राम

Today's Date :

राम
राम
राम
राम
राम
राम
राम
राम
राम
राम
राम
राम
राम
राम
राम
राम
राम
राम
राम
राम
राम
राम
राम
राम
राम
राम
राम
राम
राम
राम
राम
राम
राम
राम
राम

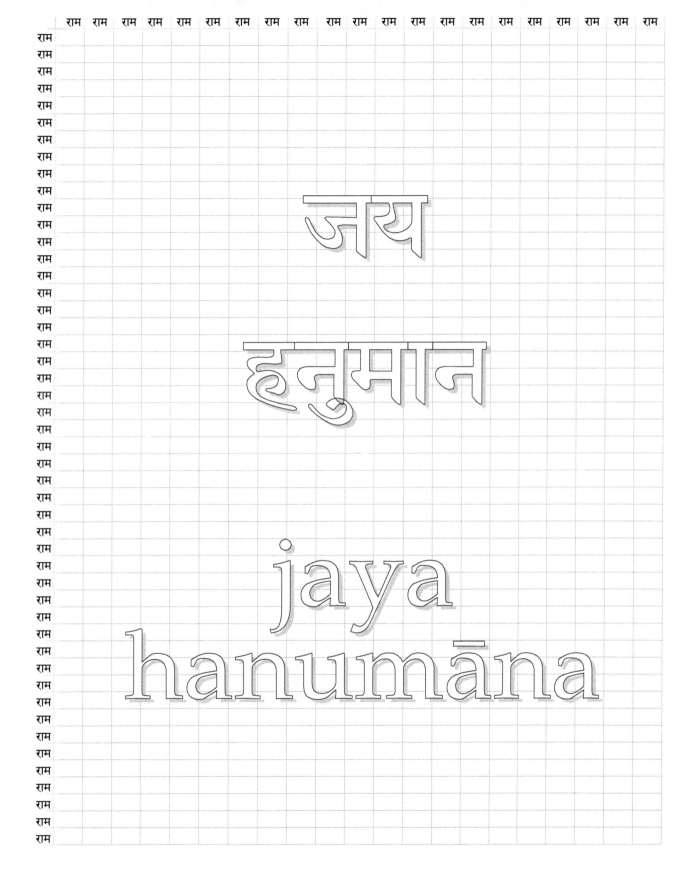

जय

हनुमान

jaya
hanumāna

जय

सीताराम

jaya
sitārāma

: Today's Date :

श्री हनुमान चालीसा
śrī-hanumāna-cālīsā

---------- दोहा - dohā ----------

श्रीगुरु चरन सरोज रज निज मन मुकुर सुधारि ।

बरनउँ रघुबर बिमल जस जो दायक फल चारि ॥

śrīguru carana saroja raja nija mana mukura sudhāri,
baranaūṁ raghubara bimala jasa jo dāyaka phala cāri.

Cleansing the mirror of mind with the dust from the lotus feet of the revered Guru, I sing the unsullied glories of Shrī Rāma—the bestower of four fruits of life.

बुद्धि हीन तनु जानिकै सुमिरौं पवन कुमार ।

बल बुद्धि बिद्या देहु मोहि हरहु कलेश विकार ॥

buddhi hīna tanu jānikai sumirauṁ pavana kumāra,
bala buddhi bidyā dehu mohi harahu kaleśa vikāra.

Knowing this material body to be void of intelligence and seeped in ignorance, I meditate on the Son-of-Wind seeking his favor: Impart to me strength, intelligence, virtuosity; and remove all ailments and imperfections, my Lord.

---------- चौपाई - caupāī ----------

जय हनुमान ज्ञान गुण सागर । जय कपीश तिहुँ लोक उजागर ॥
jaya hanumāna jñāna guṇa sāgara,
jaya kapīśa tihuṁ loka ujāgara. 1.

Glory be to Hanumān—the ocean of wisdom and virtues. Victory to the monkey-god whose resplendency irradiates the three spheres of creation.

राम दूत अतुलित बल धामा । अंजनिपुत्र पवनसुत नामा ॥
rāma dūta atulita bala dhāmā,
aṁjani-putra pavanasuta nāmā. 2.

Glory be to the divine messenger and servant of Shrī Rāma, the repository of immeasurable strength. Glory be to mother Anjani's boy, bearing the name Pavana-Suth—Son-of-Wind.

महाबीर बिक्रम बजरंगी । कुमति निवार सुमति के संगी ॥
mahābīra bikrama bajaraṁgī,
kumati nivāra sumati ke saṁgī. 3.

O supremely valorous hero of wondrous great deeds, with a body that is strong as diamond: evilness of the mind you cure; a companion you are of those with minds good and pure.

कंचन बरन बिराज सुबेषा । कानन कुंडल कुंचित केशा ॥
kaṁcana barana birāja subeṣā,
kānana kuṁḍala kuṁcita keśā. 4.

With a complexion that's molten gold, you shine resplendent in your exquisite form—with rings in your ears and lovely curly locks.

हाथ बज्र और ध्वजा बिराजै । काँधे मूँज जनेऊ साजै ॥
hātha bajra aura dhvajā birājai,
kāṁdhe mūṁja janeū sājai. 5.

In your hands are held a mace and flag; and there's *Munji* and *Janeu* embellished across your shoulders, well adorned.

शङ्कर स्वयं केशरीनंदन । तेज प्रताप महा जग बंदन ॥
śaṅkara svayaṁ keśarīnaṁdana,
teja pratāpa mahā jaga baṁdana. 6.

You are Shankar himself (embodied as Hanuman), born to the mighty Keshari—the delight of his heart. Your majesty and prowess is astounding—venerated throughout the universe.

विद्यावान गुणी अति चातुर । राम काज करिबे को आतुर ॥
vidyā-vāna guṇī ati cātura,
rāma kāja karibe ko ātura. 7.

Learned in all the sciences, virtuous, most clever and wise—you are ever so eager to do Rāma's tasks.

प्रभु चरित्र सुनिबे को रसिया । राम लखन सीता मन बसिया ॥
prabhu caritra sunibe ko rasiyā,
rāma lakhana sītā mana basiyā. 8.

Your greatest delight is in listening to the glories of the Lord, and Rāma-Lakshman-Sītā ever reside in your heart; nay—you ever abide in the hearts of Lakshman-Sītā-Rāma.

सूक्ष्म रूप धरि सियहिं दिखावा । बिकट रूप धरि लंक जरावा ॥
sūkṣma rūpa dhari siyahiṁ dikhāvā,
bikaṭa rūpa dhari laṁka jarāvā. 9.

भीम रूप धरि असुर सँहारे । रामचन्द्र के काज सँवारे ॥
bhīma rūpa dhari asura saṁhāre,
rāma-candra ke kāja saṁvāre. 10.

When visiting mother Sītā you showed yourself in tiny diminutive form; then growing to fearsome colossal size you burnt the whole of Lankā down; assuming a valorous form you destroyed many demons—thus you ever serve to facilitate the works of the Lord-God Shrī Rāma-Chandra.

लाय संजीवनि लखन जियाये । श्री रघुबीर हरषि उर लाये ॥
lāya saṁjīvani lakhana jiyāye,
śrī raghu-bīra haraṣi ura lāye. 11.

You brought the *Sanjīvani* and brought Lakshman back to life, whereupon Shrī Rāma embraced you with a heart full of joy.

रघुपति कीन्ही बहुत बड़ाई । तुम मम प्रिय भरतहिं सम भाई ॥
raghupati kīnhī bahuta baṛāī,
tuma mama priya bharatahiṁ sama bhāī. 12.

Rāma, King of Raghus, extolled you profusely and then He proclaimed: You are to me just like Bharata, dear brother of mine.

सहस बदन तुम्हरो जस गावैं । अस कहि श्रीपति कंठ लगावैं ॥
sahasa badana tumharo jasa gāvaiṁ,
asa kahi śrīpati kaṁṭha lagāvaiṁ. 13.

Thousands of beings are singing your praise—with those words to you, Rāma again to you, unto His heart did raise.

सनकादिक ब्रह्मादि मुनीशा । नारद शारद सहित अहीशा ॥
sanak-ādika brahmādi munīśā,
nārada śārada sahita ahīśā. 14.

जम कुबेर दिगपाल जहाँ ते । कबि कोबिद कहि सकै कहाँ ते ॥
jama kubera digapāla jahāṁ te,
kabi kobida kahi sakai kahāṁ te. 15.

Celibate *Rishis* like Sanaka; gods like Brahmmā; the foremost *Munis*; Nārad, Saraswatī with Shiva and Vishnu; the eight *Dikpālas* including Yama and Kubera—they all tell you glory but fail to fully delineate it; how then can mere mortals, poets and Vedic scholars sing your laurels?

तुम उपकार सुग्रीवहिं कीन्हा । राम मिलाय राज पद दीन्हा ॥
tuma upakāra sugrīvahiṁ kīnhā,
rāma milāya rāja pada dīnhā. 16.

You bestowed favor upon Sugrīva—you brought him near to Rāma and made him the King of Kishkindhā.

तुम्हरो मंत्र बिभीषन माना । लंकेश्वर भए सब जग जाना ॥
tumharo maṁtra bibhīṣana mānā,
laṁkeśvara bhae saba jaga jānā. 17.

Vibhīshan accepted your Mantra, and as consequence became the King of Lankā—this is well known throughout the world.

जुग सहस्र जोजन पर भानु । लील्यो ताहि मधुर फल जानू ॥
* juga sahastra jojana para bhānū,
līlyo tāhi madhura phala jānū. 18.

At a thousand *Yuga Yojan* is the Sun, and mistaking it for a sweet fruit, you supped it up—while still an infant.

प्रभु मुद्रिका मेलि मुख माहीं । जलधि लाँघि गये अचरज नाहीं ॥
prabhu mudrikā meli mukha māhīṁ,
jaladhi lāṁghi gaye acaraja nāhīṁ. 19.

The ring of the Lord you placed in your mouth and then leaped across the ocean to give it to Sītā. But what wonder is there in that? [Verily, scaling the impossible comes to you with ease.]

दुर्गम काज जगत के जेते । सुगम अनुग्रह तुम्हरे तेते ॥
durgama kāja jagata ke jete,
sugama anugraha tumhare tete. 20.

All the difficult tasks of the world become easy were it your pleasure—if there, O Lord, be the favor of your grace.

राम दुआरे तुम रखवारे । होत न आज्ञा बिनु पैसारे ॥
rāma duāre tuma rakhavāre,
hota na ājñā binu paisāre. 21.

You are the keeper and protector of doorway to Rāma; without your command, nobody can enter the abode of Shrī Rāma.

सब सुख लहैं तुम्हारी शरना । तुम रक्षक काहू को डर ना ॥

**saba sukha lahaiṁ tumhārī śaranā,
tuma rakṣaka kāhū ko ḍara nā. 22.**

Every happiness abides with those who bide under your protection. With you as one's guardian, there is never any cause of fear.

आपन तेज सम्हारो आपै । तीनौं लोक हाँक ते काँपै ॥

**āpana teja samhāro āpai,
tīnauṁ loka hāṁka te kāṁpai. 23.**

You alone can withstand your own splendor; verily the three worlds quake when your thunder.

भूत पिशाच निकट नहिं आवै । महाबीर जब नाम सुनावै ॥

**bhūta piśāca nikaṭa nahiṁ āvai,
mahābīra jaba nāma sunāvai. 24.**

Evil spirits and ghosts dare come near not: when the chant of Mahābira—your name—is invoked.

नासै रोग हरै सब पीरा । जपत निरंतर हनुमत बीरा ॥

**nāsai roga harai saba pīrā,
japata niraṁtara hanumata bīrā. 25.**

All diseases are destroyed, all pains are ended—with the constant chant of the Name 'Hanumān', the Brave-Supreme.

संकट ते हनुमान छुड़ावै । मन क्रम बचन ध्यान जो लावै ॥

**saṁkaṭa te hanumāna churāvai,
mana krama bacana dhyāna jo lāvai. 26.**

Lord Hanumān removes all afflictions, every adversity—for those who remember him in heart, word & deed.

सब पर राम तपस्वी राजा । तिन के काज सकल तुम साजा ॥

**saba para rāma tapasvī rājā,
tina ke kāja sakala tuma sājā. 27.**

Rāma, the Ascetic-King, is the sovereign ruler over all; and it is you who administer his works.

और मनोरथ जो कोउ लावै । तासु अमित जीवन फल पावै ॥

**aura manoratha jo kou lāvai,
tāsu amita jīvana phala pāvai. 28.**

When one comes to you with a heart's desire, you yield unto him unlimited fruits for the whole life in entire.

चारों जुग परताप तुम्हारा । है परसिद्ध जगत उजियारा ॥

**cāroṁ juga paratāpa tumhārā,
hai parasiddha jagata ujiyārā. 29.**

Your resplendency persists across all the times; in all the four *Yugas*, your fame illumines throughout the universe.

साधु संत के तुम रखवारे । असुर निकंदन राम दुलारे ॥

**sādhu saṁta ke tuma rakhavāre,
asura nikaṁdana rāma dulāre. 30.**

You—dear-most son of Rāma—are the guardian of the saintly, virtuous, wise; and you are the destroyer of the fiends and the vile.

अष्ट सिद्धि नव निधि के दाता । अस बर दीन्ह जानकी माता ॥

**aṣṭa siddhi nava nidhi ke dātā,
asa bara dīnha jānakī mātā. 31.**

You are the bestower of all eight *Siddhis* and nine *Nidhis*—Mother Sītā, daughter of Janak, herself endowed you with that power.

राम रसायन तुम्हरे पासा । सदा रहउ रघुपति के दासा ॥

**rāma rasāyana tumhare pāsā,
sadā rahau raghupati ke dāsā. 32.**

You own the sweet treasure of devotion to Rāma; you ever abide as the foremost attendant of that Jewel of Rhagu scion.

तुम्हरे भजन राम को पावै । जनम जनम के दुख बिसरावै ॥

**tumhare bhajana rāma ko pāvai,
janama janama ke dukha bisarāvai. 33.**

अंत काल रघुबर पुर जाई । जहाँ जन्म हरिभक्त कहाई ॥

**aṁta kāla raghubara pura jāī,
jahāṁ janma haribhakta kahāī. 34.**

Through devotion to you one is able to obtain to the Lord; and the adversities and afflictions of millions of births become defeated thereupon; and at the time of their end, one goes to Rāma's own abode—remaining there eternally as Rāma's very own.

और देवता चित्त न धरई । हनुमत सेइ सर्ब सुख करई ॥

**aura devatā citta na dharaī,
hanumata sei sarba sukha karaī. 35.**

Swearing by no other god, and just serving Shrī Hanumān alone—one obtains every happiness in this world and the next.

संकट कटै मिटै सब पीरा । जो सुमिरै हनुमत बलबीरा ॥

**saṁkaṭa kaṭai miṭai saba pīrā,
jo sumirai hanumata balabīrā. 36.**

All troubles are cut short, all pains removed—for they who meditate upon Hanumān, the mighty, brave, supreme.

जय जय जय हनुमान गोसाई । कृपा करहु गुरु देव की नाई ॥
**jaya jaya jaya hanumāna gosāīṁ,
kṛpā karahu guru deva kī nāīṁ.** 37.
Victory to you Hanumān, O master of senses. May you remain ever victorious, ever triumphant. Shower your grace upon us—as lovingly as a Guru does.

यह शत बार पाठ कर जोई । छूटै बंदि महा सुख सोई ॥
**yaha śata bāra pāṭha kara joī,
chūṭai baṁdi mahā sukha soī.** 38.
One who recites this Hanumān Chālīsā a hundred times is released from all bondages and obtains bliss everlasting.

जो यह पढ़ै हनुमान चालीसा । होय सिद्धि साखी गौरीसा ॥
**jo yaha paṛhai hanumāna cālīsā,
hoya siddhi sākhī gaurīsā.** 39.
One who reads this Hanumān Chālīsā becomes a *Siddha*—Gaurī's Lord Shiva himself bears witness to that.

तुलसीदास सदा हरि चेरा । कीजै नाथ हृदय महँ डेरा ॥
**tulasī-dāsa sadā hari cerā,
kījai nātha hṛdaya mahaṁ ḍerā.** 40.
Tulsīdās is ever a disciple of Shrī Rāma; O Lord Hanumān, do please take up thy abode in my heart as well.

---------- दोहा - dohā ----------

पवन तनय संकट हरन मंगल मूरति रूप ।
pavana tanaya saṁkaṭa harana maṁgala mūrati rūpa,

राम लखन सीता सहित हृदय बसहु सुर भूप ॥
rāma lakhana sītā sahita hṛdaya basahu sura bhūpa.

O Son-of-Wind, remover of all disasters & sin—O Radiant-One, of the most auspicious visage—may you ever and ever abide within my heart—along with Lakshman, Sītā, Rāma—O first amongst all gods.

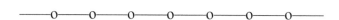

* The distance to Sun (***Bhānū***) is being given out in the 18th Chaupai as 96 million miles (12,000x1000x8). ***Juga*** (which equal 12,000 Divine-Years as per Vedic-Time-Scale) is used as a number here; ***sahastra*** means 1000; ***jojana*** is a distance of 8 miles. This distance to Sun—which is within 3.3% of modern day calculations—in mere three simple words (***juga sahastra jojana***), given out by Tulsīdās from sixteenth century India, is remarkable; for it not only shows what all our ancients knew way, way back; but it also demonstrates Tulsīdās' dexterity in choosing the right succinct words throughout his poesy.

(Author of this Original Devanāgrī Hymn is: Goswamī Tulsīdās [16th Century Saint]. Translator: Sushma)

Our next Journals in the series are available:
Rama Jayam - Likhita Japam :: Rama-Nama Mala Upon **Nama Ramayanam**
Rama Jayam - Likhita Japam :: Rama-Nama Mala Upon **Rama 108 Names**
Rama Jayam - Likhita Japam :: Rama-Nama Mala Upon **Rama Raksha Stotra**
...more on the way. For latest, please see *www.onlyRama.com*